MIND RIGHT

MIND RIGHT

by
Lorraine Phillips

360 Books, LLC
Atlanta, GA

Thank you for purchasing this book. If you find it to be helpful, then please kindly leave a quick review on Amazon. Your help in spreading the word is much appreciated.

The link is: http://bit.ly/mind-right

Thank you.

To download FREE uplifting, inspirational products, please visit:

www. mind right book .com

Cover and interior design by Lorraine Phillips.

Copyright © 2017 by Lorraine Phillips.

All rights reserved. No part of this book may be reproduced or transmitted in any form by any means whether graphic, electronic, or mechanical, including photocopying, recording, taping, or by any information storage or retrieval system without prior written permission from the publisher.

The purpose of this book is to inform, educate, and entertain. Although every precaution has been taken in preparation of this book, there may be errors, both typographical and in content. The publisher and author assume no responsibility for any errors or omissions. Neither is any liability assumed for damages resulting, directly or indirectly, from the use of the information contained herein.

Author: Lorraine Phillips
Website: www.lorraine-phillips.com
Email: mindright@lorraine-phillips.com

Editor: Marilyn Burkley

ISBN-10: 0-9822765-8-3
ISBN-13: 978-0-9822765-8-7

LCCN: 2017905755
Library of Congress subject headings:
1) Spiritual life 2) Spirituality 3) Self Help 4) New Thought 5) Metaphysical

Published by 360 Books, LLC.

First Printing.
Printed in the United States of America.

This is dedicated to AR. I promise that your best is yet to come. I pray that what you have in your hands will serve as a manifesto and guide you can use to get there. I can't wait till this world gets to see all you have to offer. It is going to be absolutely amazing.

Mark my words!

Acknowledgments

To Lewis, Lera, and Leon (my "L" family) thanks for always watching over me.

Thanks to the elders who paved the way: my mother, Veronica Holly, Cherry Igbinedion, and Henrietta Girard.

A big thank you goes out to my UK massive, namely, Victoria Girard, Cherry B, Sharon Sylvester, and Sandra Smith.

The same goes for my US crew, namely, Josette Jeffers, Kim Perdue-Sims, Sylvia Copeland, Dee McDonald, and my spiritual mother, Omolewa Eniolorunopa.

I would also like to shout out my local Alpharetta Starbucks where 99.9 percent of this was written. Thanks to Emma, Mason, Amy, Lauren, Meghan, Ashley, Devante, Naomi, Renee, Kalii, and the rest of the team for their excellent display of Southern hospitality. I mean, it got to the point where they'd have my drink ready as soon as I pulled up. It just doesn't get any better than that!

And lastly, a big thanks to all those who helped me realize the importance of writing and sharing a book such as this and who kept me encouraged along the way. You know who you are!

The ultimate solution to any problem lies within your thinking, because what happens in your mind determines your experience of life.
~ Marianne Williamson

Table of Contents

Introduction...17

Part I: Understanding Your Mind

Chapter 1: The Power Inside Your Mind..............................21
Chapter 2: The Different States of the Brain.......................25
Chapter 3: The Power of Your Underlying Beliefs..............29
Chapter 4: What Are You "Attracting" into Your Life?.......35
Chapter 5: Your Reticular Activating System......................39
Chapter 6: Reprogramming Your Beliefs.............................43

Part II: About You

Chapter 7: Who Are You and Why Are You Here?.............49
Chapter 8: The Nine Types of Intelligence..........................57
Chapter 9: Your Statement of Purpose................................61

Part III: Laying the Foundation

Chapter 10: Foundation Basics 101.......................................71
    Monitor Your Thoughts...71
    Let Go of Past Hurts and Disappointment..............73
    Get Rid of Toxic People..76
    Find Your Cheerleaders...77
Chapter 11: Foundation Basics 102 79
    Eliminate Worry and Fear...79
    There's No Such Thing as Failure............................82

Take Responsibility for Your Life..........................84
Clear the Clutter..85
Chapter 12: Controlling the Theater in Your Mind............87
Chapter 13: How We Learn...91

Part IV: Steps to Transforming Your Life

Chapter 14: Surrender..97
Chapter 15: Meditate..103
Two Simple Meditation Techniques..........................105
Chanting..107
A Few Mantras and Their Meanings............110
Binaural Beats, Your Shortcut to Meditation............115
Chapter 16: Set Your Intentions..117
Example Intentions..118
Chapter 17: Have an Attitude of Gratitude.......................123
Chapter 18: Affirm..127
Tips and Guidelines for Creating Your Script.........130
Making Your Affirmation Powerful.........................133
A Sample Script..138
Record It..140
Chapter 19: Visualize..145
Create a Video...149
Chapter 20: Afform...153
Chapter 21: Celebrate Yourself..157
Chapter 22: Take Action..161
Chapter 23: BONUS Chapter: 12 Ways to Stay Motivated on Your Journey..165

Resources
    Recommended Reads and Classics.......................177
    Websites for Guided Meditations............................185
About the Author...187

Introduction

It's so weird, I always end up writing a book's introduction at the very end of the process and not the beginning as you would expect. The reason the introduction always ends up being last is because, although I start out writing with a basic notion of what I'd like to create, I have absolutely no idea of where it will end up—you see, I leave those kinds of details to something that is much bigger, smarter, and wiser than me. My only job is to simply get out of the way—as you will learn to do and understand more about once you begin practicing some of the exercises presented in the steps to transforming your life.

Much like you, I found myself in a position in life where I had to ask myself, "How on earth did I get here?" And so, my investigation began. Everything happens for a reason, and if I had not been in the place I was, then this journey would never have begun.

Herein lies the quest I undertook for self-discovery and exploration. Not being someone who blames their outer circumstances on…well, outer circumstances, I have always realized my ability to take full responsibility for absolutely everything that happens in my life, and I know enough to know that over time I can change anything I want.

As I began the process of deep introspection, much knowledge and wisdom was imparted to me. Information flew to me from all directions, literally at warp speed. You may call it synchronicity—but because I had the courage to ask, I received in abundance.

I was truly amazed by what I discovered, and was so excited that I began to share this information with family and friends. We would talk on the phone for hours on end, and I found myself having the same conversation with different people, over and over again. I came to realize that we were all very much in the same position: wanting more, knowing we could do and be more, but uncertain about exactly what that "more" could be—and even more daunting was the question of how to get there.

I prayed and prayed for direction, and what you are about to read is what manifested as a result of my desires. My intention is to share everything I learned so that you too may benefit from this information. The concepts are simple in nature, but do not for one minute underestimate their power to get you from where you are to where you want to be. I have finally found my calling—and I did it by following the steps in this book. My hope is that you too will find your calling, so that you might lead an authentic life of intention and purpose.

Remember to have fun with all of this and enjoy the process of creating your own exceptional life—after all, that's exactly what you were born to do. You are about to become a conscious creator, where you get to live your life by design instead of by default.

I *truly* enjoyed every minute of writing this book and wish you much success in obtaining a peaceful, joyous, prosperous, love-filled, creative, free, and more meaningful life!

Lorraine Phillips, Author

Part I

Understanding Your Mind

Chapter 1

The Power Inside Your Mind

The human brain is undoubtedly the most powerful, sophisticated "machine" on the planet. Weighing less than three pounds, it is the centerpiece of your nervous system and the most complex organ in your body. Your brain represents about 2 percent of your total body weight but uses more than 20 percent of the calories you consume, 25 percent of the total blood flow in your body, and 20 percent of the oxygen you breathe. These statistics alone signal the importance of brain function and why we need to hone in and use its inherent power to help us achieve some of the things we want out of life.

Your brain has approximately 86 billion active neurons (or nerve cells), each of which can have up to 10,000 synaptic connections (or passages) that allow nerve impulses to transmit and process information. These connections are continuously being made and unmade and form a vast, ever-changing neural network in the brain.

Neuroplasticity is a term that describes the brain's ability to change throughout life. Luckily for you, your brain is wired with an amazing ability to reorganize itself and modify its existing neural network. Whenever you learn something new, your brain alters its physical structure and functional organization in a way that allows you to absorb the new information. The more you think in a certain manner, the easier it becomes to generate those types of thoughts. With regular repetition, these new thought patterns become so ingrained that they eventually become the brain's automatic way of thinking.

It is estimated that the adult brain contains one quadrillion (1,000,000,000,000,000) synapses, indicating the level of brain computing power available to you every single day, and demonstrating that your innate capacity to use your mind to achieve anything you want is virtually unlimited. Amazingly enough, there are more synapses in your brain than there are stars in the galaxy—imagine that!

In addition, your mind is made up of two parts, the conscious and the subconscious. Your conscious mind is responsible for reasoning and comprehension. It is the ordinary waking, thinking state of mind, meaning that whenever you are aware of what you are doing—or about to do—the action is being handled by your conscious. Put your right hand in the air, tap your feet, blink twice—all these actions are governed by your conscious. You are reading this now using your conscious. It is also the little chatterbox you hear constantly talking to you throughout the day.

Your subconscious mind functions just below your level of awareness (hence the term "sub" conscious). It remembers absolutely every experience you've ever had—forever. It is the part of your mind responsible for all your involuntary actions, functioning as the storehouse for all your life experiences, memories, images, skills, automatic movements, patterns, habits, attitudes, emotions, and beliefs. The subconscious mind's primary function is to learn and automatically run the stored programs that reside in it, allowing your conscious mind to be free to focus on other things.

Have you ever driven home and not even remembered how you got there? That was your subconscious in action. Once you master the skill of driving, every time you jump into the driver's seat the "driving program" that is held within your subconscious is automatically initiated. It quietly runs in the background of your mind, leaving your conscious free to focus elsewhere to the point where you literally drive without even thinking about it.

Your subconscious is always "switched on," even when you are asleep. What do you think controls your breathing, heartbeat, digestive system…as a matter of fact, all your biological functions? Yes, your subconscious—there is absolutely no way you could consciously be responsible for controlling all that.

To understand the relationship between your conscious and subconscious, answer the following question: what is five multiplied by six? I'll allow a few extra seconds for those who may need it. The answer is thirty, and as long as you didn't use a calculator to get the answer then you just used your conscious to access and retrieve information that's permanently stored within your subconscious.

By itself, your conscious mind is very limited in both capacity and capability. To understand just how powerful your subconscious is in comparison, consider this: your conscious mind processes about forty bits of information per second, while your subconscious is estimated to process about eleven million bits of information per second. Astounding!

Chapter 2

The Different States of The Brain

Your brain emits five different types of electrical signals (or brain wave patterns) across its cortex. It's important to understand each of these frequencies, because, as we will discuss in part IV, three of them, the *alpha, theta,* and *gamma* states, are most conducive to various mind-programming techniques that will allow you to overcome your limiting thoughts and beliefs. Electroencephalography (EEG) technology is used to measure the speed and frequency of the wave signals from one neurological point to another via electrodes attached to the surface of the scalp. The five frequencies that have been discovered thus far are categorized as follows:

Gamma (40 Hz–100 Hz)

A recent discovery in the field of neuroscience, gamma waves are the fastest frequency, measuring above 40 Hz. John Kounios of Drexel University and Mark Beeman of Northwestern University concluded that insight solutions, or "Aha!" moments, are positively correlated with bursts of gamma waves. Other benefits of this frequency include better recall, enhanced thought processing, increased intellect, improved focus, the feeling of being in "the flow," a higher level of compassion, and increased feelings of happiness. This particular frequency can be induced by brain wave entrainment using binaural beats, as will be discussed in chapter 15.

Beta (12 Hz–40 Hz)

The beta state is our normal everyday waking state where we are highly alert and focused. All forms of action—thinking, talking, problem-solving—and any negative emotions we experience, such as anger or fear, take place in the beta state. This state is not conducive to deep learning or imprinting. Too much of this frequency can make you feel stressed or anxious. According to the book *Unleashing Your Brilliance* by Brian E. Walsh, in this state a suggestion must be repeated thousands of times in order for a behavioral change to take place.

Alpha (8 Hz–12 Hz)

This is the brain's relaxed meditative state, associated with peak creativity, heightened memory, and concentration. In this state the mind is clear and highly receptive to learning new information. The alpha state is experienced while daydreaming or fantasizing, and it is also the drowsy state you undergo right before going to sleep at night or on awakening in the morning. Alpha waves are strongest when your eyes are closed. This state quiets the constant chatter of the conscious mind, allowing for direct access to the subconscious. In the alpha state a suggestion must be repeated twenty-one times in order to change a behavior, making it the ideal time for reprogramming the mind using the various techniques presented in part IV of this book.

Theta (4 Hz–8 Hz)

Theta waves are associated with dreaming and light sleep. This relaxed semi-hypnotic state allows for deep meditation and high access to the subconscious. In this state a suggestion must be repeated only once or twice for a change in behavior to take place.

Delta (0.1 Hz–4 Hz)

These are the slowest of the brain wave patterns, produced when there is a total loss of body awareness as occurs during deep sleep, in a coma state, or under general anesthesia. In this state the pituitary gland triggers the release of growth hormones that are beneficial to natural healing and cell regeneration.

Chapter 3

The Power of Your Underlying Beliefs

The beliefs you have right now are the views you hold to be true about yourself and the world around you, although not necessarily based in truth at all. Beliefs are just repeated thoughts that are so ingrained in your mind that they have become stored programs that are automatically run by your subconscious. Beliefs can also emerge instantaneously as a result of a one-time learning experience, as in the case of a suddenly developed phobia or something of that nature.

The basis of your underlying belief systems was actually formed during early childhood—between the ages of two and twelve—and were most likely passed down to you by your parents, teachers, family members, religious leaders, books and other media, experiences, culture, and any other significant or influential entities of the time. Whether you constantly heard statements like "You'll never amount to anything," "You're so stupid," or things like "You're smart, you can do it," and "You're such a handsome young man," these comments, more than likely, still affect your life today.

Although you may think that most actions and behaviors are controlled by our conscious minds, studies indicate that almost 90 percent of our daily activities are actually regulated by our subconscious, meaning that most of our patterns of behavior are automated and not as spontaneous as we think. Remember the story of the *Titanic*? Only 10 percent of that iceberg was visible, but it's what was beneath the surface—the other 90 percent—that actually destroyed the ship. And your underlying beliefs can do the same to you. Limiting, self-defeating beliefs hold you back as they run like a virus in the background of your mind. Most people spend too much time trying to fix their outer reality, not realizing that their outer reality is just a projection of what's going on inside their minds.

> **He who looks outside dreams,**
> **he who looks inside awakes.**
> ~ Carl Jung

Let me give you an example of something I discovered about myself when I was much younger. I considered myself to be multi-talented and was very good at what I did. I always commanded a high salary in the workplace, but when it came to doing the things I loved and enjoyed, I was never able to make a decent living out of it. Whatever happened to "Do what you love and the money will follow"? I certainly was doing what I loved, but…

The last straw came when a gentleman for whom I had designed a website literally disappeared when it was time for him to pay up. Since this client had been introduced by a close friend, I had neglected to collect the 50 percent up-front fee, as was my normal business practice. The gentleman had seen the site, and I could tell was very impressed. Not only that, but the patrons around us oohed and aahed as I showed him the final design—so I think it's safe to say that my work was not in question here. So, instead of getting upset about the situation, I decided to take a look at myself to understand why I kept attracting those particular types of clients—you know, the ones who develop a blank stare as soon as you mention money, almost as if they had expected me to work for free.

I did a little delving, and one day out of the blue it hit me. What had I always said while working wholeheartedly on those outside projects? I couldn't count the number of times I had said, "I'm not doing it for the money." It was just that simple. And as a result, I never made good money from doing the things I loved to do (back then). That lightning bolt of revelation inspired me to examine other areas of my life where I was not consistently producing the things I had boldly stated I wanted, and in almost every situation I found an undermining belief there also.

Believe it or not (no pun intended), your beliefs are ingrained thoughts that govern your very existence. You think with your conscious mind, but your beliefs (and automatic programs) are held within your subconscious. If you're thinking to yourself with your conscious, "Oh, I'd really love to get that promotion," but your underlying belief is "I don't deserve the position. I haven't been to college, I don't have a degree, and I'm not smart enough for the job," guess which thought ultimately creates your reality? Your world is not governed by what you *say*, it's governed by what you *believe* (deep down, regardless of what you say), and what you believe then determines what you make true. In summary, your life is just a reflection of your beliefs. A person who *believes* they can achieve anything they put their mind to will act very differently from a person who *believes* they will not succeed at most things.

> **For as he thinketh in his heart, so is he.**
> ~ Proverbs 23:7

Not all of your beliefs are bad guys, and most actually work in your favor, but the ones that don't constantly sabotage your efforts to achieve the things you want in life. So how do you know which beliefs are serving you and which are not? Take a look at the results you're producing in different areas of your life—I can tell you, without a shadow of a doubt, that your absolute underlying belief is (or was) your result.

To discover some of the limiting beliefs you may have, fill in the blanks of these sentences to highlight self-defeating statements you have made. Try to think back and remember the last time you used these phrases and exactly what you said.

I would_____
but _____

I could_____
but _____

I wish I could_____
but _____

I'd like to_____
but _____

I can't_____
because _____

There is no way I can_____
because _____

Now look at the list of limiting beliefs you just created. Dig deeper into each one and try to figure out what fear you have linked to that belief. What thoughts are you associating with each that makes it *seem* true? Do you know where the limiting belief came from? More importantly, who would you be without that belief? What actions would you take? What changes would you make? What is the exact opposite of any of the sentences you created above?

From now on you must always challenge your limiting beliefs. Ask yourself, is this really true? Is it a fact or just a belief? Is this just my imagination playing with me? Is this true for all people on the planet—and if that is not the case, what makes it (seem) true for only me? The more you ask these types of questions that challenge and get to the bottom of these beliefs, the weaker they will become. Keep digging and go deep enough until you get to the point where you can expose and debunk them all as merely debilitating myths.

Chapter 4

What Are You "Attracting" into Your Life?

Einstein proved that everything is made up of energy and that all energy vibrates at a certain level or frequency. We too then—as humans—are balls of energy that vibrate at a frequency according to the level of our thoughts, feelings, *and* beliefs.

Ever meet somebody for the first time and find your spirit just taking to them right away? What about the exact opposite, where you met someone and immediately didn't like or trust them for no apparent reason? How about this: have you ever walked into a room where folks had just had an argument, unbeknownst to you, but it felt like you could cut the tension with a knife? If you've experienced any of those types of situations then you were simply picking up on a vibe, or vibration. And the things that are going on in your life right now, whether good or bad, are operating on the same principle.

What's showing up in your life are the things you constantly give your energy, focus, and attention to. People, situations, and circumstances are showing up that match your "vibe," whether you're emitting a "high" or a "low" vibration. Ever wonder why bad things keep happening to that friend of yours who's constantly filled with doom and gloom, or why your happy-go-lucky friend is, well, so happy *and* lucky?

If you're constantly thinking negative thoughts and complaining about the things you don't have, then you'll end up attracting more negativity into your life. It's not simply about holding positive thoughts (there's much more to it than that, as we will discover), but if you constantly think about the things that are currently *working* in your life, then you stand to attract more of those types of situations and circumstances. Just being in a more positive (and grateful) vibration means that you are—at the very least—more open to positive outcomes, and sometimes that's all you really need. If there's a mechanism that already works in this world and has been built to function that way, why on earth would you want to buck the trend and disrupt its flow?

> **Everything is energy and that's all there is to it. Match the frequency of the reality you want and you cannot help but get that reality. It can be no other way. This is not philosophy. This is physics.**
> ~ Albert Einstein

Let's suppose that your favorite show comes on channel 12 at 8:30 p.m. You get all prepared: you have snacks in hand, your favorite beverage, comfy PJs, and you're ready to go. But if your TV is tuned to channel 7 then there is no way you can catch the show that's playing on channel 12. Even though your TV is able to receive the signal from channel 12, you simply won't receive it, because you are tuned to an entirely different channel (or in our case, frequency).

You have to train your mind in a way that allows you to raise your thoughts to match the level of the vibration of the things you would like in life. By adjusting your frequency (as in the example above, switching over to channel 12), you align yourself with the things you want and put yourself in a position where you can actually receive them.

Have you ever wondered why 75 percent of multi-million-dollar lottery winners end up worse off than they were before their big win? It's because they were not prepared for their newfound wealth and had not yet become the people they needed to be (in terms of the level of vibration) to sustain that level of income. That's why it's important to prepare yourself for the things you want and start acting as if they're here, right now, before they even get here.

Understanding that like attracts like, you can literally attract anything you want into your life just by finding different ways to raise your vibration. Here are some examples of positive and negative states of being (or levels of vibration) that can serve to either attract or block you from receiving the things you want.

Positive	Negative
Loving	Hateful
Thankful	Ungrateful
Joyous	Sorrowful
Selfless	Selfish
Creative	Uninspired
Powerful	Insignificant
Generous	Greedy
Courageous	Fearful
Decisive	Indecisive
Peaceful	Worried
Content	Jealous
Happy	Sad
Hopeful	Despairing
Satisfied	Frustrated
Calm	Angry
Compassionate	Merciless
Forgiving	Revengeful
Confident	Doubtful
Interested	Bored
Harmonious	Conflicted
Accepted	Rejected
Free	Enslaved
Strong	Weak

Chapter 5

Your Reticular Activating System

As read previously, your subconscious mind processes over eleven million bits of information per second. However, you are only consciously aware of about two thousand of those. Your reticular activating system (RAS) is a network of densely packed neural fibers. It's approximately the size of your little finger and is located at the base of your brain stem. This control center acts as a filter within your brain, processing all information in the "background" of your mind before deciding which information it should present to you by way of your conscious mind.

Think Google for a moment. Imagine we did a search for…well, let's say the "reticular activating system." Although there would be literally thousands of results, Google would only display what it considered to be the most relevant (and accurate) on the first page. Despite the fact that every search result Google could find would be there and listed on subsequent pages, it is extremely unlikely that you would ever see those results. Our minds function in exactly the same manner—sandwiching up data into easy, convenient, relevant bits of information in a way that's just enough for us to handle and prevent information overload.

Have you ever purchased a brand-new car and thought you had the only one on the road, but as soon as you wheeled out of the dealership you noticed that everywhere you looked you saw black Honda Civics? Or have you been at a noisy party totally engrossed in a conversation, when all of a sudden—as clear as day—you hear your name mentioned from way across the room? How do you think a mother is able to distinguish the cry of her baby in a room full of screaming children? Your RAS is responsible for constantly filtering and presenting the information that appears on your "high priority list" and calling your attention to those items. It decides what information is important and what can safely be ignored. The black Honda Civics didn't just appear out of nowhere—they were always there, but you hadn't noticed them yet because they were not on your high priority list.

As you see, we tend to only notice the things that are important or relevant to us. A fashion stylist will always pay attention to the way people dress, an optometrist to the eyeglasses people wear—and a cop will always be on the lookout for shady-looking characters even while he's supposedly relaxing at the neighborhood cookout.

Your RAS knows what to present according to the things you focus on or pay more attention to. Reprogramming your mind (which means changing the automatic programs that are currently being run by your subconscious) lets your RAS know exactly what items to add to your high priority list so it can find and present the most relevant information to you accordingly. It sorts through data based on the similar patterns that already exist in your brain, and any evidence it finds that is contrary to what already exists is simply disregarded. That's why it's so important for you to zoom in and focus on the things you want in life rather than the things you don't.

Now you understand why bad things are always happening to Ms. Doom and Gloom. There are actually a lot of good things going on for her as well, but due to her constant focus on negative situations, her RAS is now programmed to literally ignore the good stuff and instead zoom in on situations that are most in line with her current way of (negative) thinking. This may also explain why your happy-go-lucky friend somehow usually manages to remain charged, positive, and upbeat regardless of the circumstances.

As another example: if you constantly focus on the fact that love always seems to elude you, then when Mr. or Ms. Right finally shows up, you likely won't notice. Due to your underlying thought pattern, your RAS will disregard Mr. or Ms. Right's approaches, while it continues to go on the hunt to deliver supporting evidence of your underlying belief—to the point where what you believe eventually becomes a self-fulfilling prophecy.

Armed with the right information, you will be surprised at how quickly your RAS can help you attract people, situations, circumstances, and events that can aid in the fulfillment of your dreams.

Chapter 6

Reprogramming Your Beliefs

So let's do a quick recap. The beliefs that control most of your actions reside within your subconscious—below the level of consciousness. They were, for the most part, deposited there by others during your youth, and by now are so old and deeply hidden that you don't even really know what they are. Your job now is to rewire your thoughts in a way that allows the brain to release the self-limiting beliefs (some of which we identified in chapter 3) and replace them with new beliefs that allow you to surpass any limitations you thought you ever had.

> **Progress is impossible without change, and those who cannot change their minds cannot change anything.**
> ~ George Bernard Shaw

Reprogramming the underlying beliefs held within your subconscious will involve creating mental pictures that integrate positive thoughts into your belief system as *truth*, allowing for internal change that produces external results. All the positive thoughts in the world won't change anything unless you can first successfully integrate them into your system as truth.

> **What we think, we become.**
> ~ Buddha

Know that your subconscious does not think, reason, judge, critique, or rationalize. It is a willing "servant" that readily submits to any training it is given and is so competent that scientists have not yet been able to find a single thing along mental lines that it cannot do.

Andrew Carnegie once gave a speech in which he said that everyone comes to the earth blessed with the privilege of controlling his mind power and directing it to whatever heights he would like it to reach. He went on to say that everyone also brings along with them two sealed envelopes, one labeled "the riches you may enjoy if you take possession of your own mind," and the other labeled "the penalties you must pay if you fail to take possession of your mind." According to Mr. Carnegie, the envelope labeled "riches" contained the following:

- Sound health
- Peace of mind
- A labor of love of your own choice

- Freedom from fear and worry
- A positive mental attitude
- Material riches of your own choice and quantity

The second envelope labeled "penalties," contained the following:

- Ill health
- Fear and worry
- Indecision and doubt
- Frustration and discouragement throughout life
- Poverty and want
- A whole flock of evils including envy, greed, jealousy, anger, hatred, and superstition

I know which envelope I wish to partake of, and you must, too, otherwise you would not be reading this book. Ultimately, we would like to *magnetize* situations, circumstances, people, events, and ideas that allow us to achieve our aspirations. But before we move into the mind programming techniques presented in part IV, we need to delve a little further into exactly who you are and why you are here. Let's go!

> **Knowing yourself
> is the beginning of all wisdom.**
> ~ Aristotle

Part II

About You

Chapter 7

Who Are You and Why Are You Here?

> Your purpose on this planet is to
> become who you are. That's it!
> ~ Author Unknown

How many of us can answer the questions "Who are you?" and "Why are you here?" without a moment's hesitation? It's highly unlikely that you'd be reading this book if you could, but that's the reason we're on this journey together. It's easy for you to name your boss, the car you drive, your favorite food... but your reason for being—not so simple.

If we're completely honest, most of us feel that there is some unique purpose for our life. We know there's something we were born to do that we've been uniquely prepared for, even if it feels like we haven't quite found (or stumbled across) that elusive "it" yet.

Deep down inside, you know you were created for greatness, and you hunger to be awoken from what feels like a mundane, routine existence and instead lead a life of passion, freedom, fulfillment, and possibly even joy. Imagine that! Would you believe me if I told you that you already have *everything* you need to succeed? Up until now, you've looked outside of yourself for fulfillment, but *true* fulfillment can only come from within.

> **As long as we focus on the outside, there will always be that empty, hungry, lost place inside that needs to be filled.**
> ~ Shakti Gawain

The following questions will help you discover for yourself who you are and why you are here, providing a clearer vision of what your purpose may be and putting you into a position that allows you to create a sense of direction and meaning in your life. Take time to answer *all* the questions. Not to be melodramatic, but this could possibly be one of the most important things you do in life, so be totally honest with yourself. If you have trouble answering any of the questions, consult a trusted friend for help; you know they will always have an answer for you. This section may seem lengthy, but unfortunately, there are no shortcuts in creating a life you love.

> **Only by much searching and mining are gold and diamonds obtained.**
> ~ James Allen

Find a time when you can be relaxed and at peace. It is unlikely that you will finish everything in one sitting, but please do not move on to subsequent chapters until this is complete. This is a building process for which we are about to lay the foundation. I suggest you start by writing your answers here and then rewriting them in a personal notebook, because simply performing the action twice lets you begin practicing mind reprogramming techniques right away.

> **The unexamined life is not worth living.**
> ~ Socrates

Please note that the following set of questions can be also downloaded from www.mindrightbook.com.

Answer the following:
What is different, special, or unique about you?

What do friends always compliment you on or tell you you're good at?

What qualities do you admire most about yourself?

Name three of your greatest achievements:
1.

2.

3.

What did you do for fun as a child?

What did you say you wanted to be when you grew up? Why?

What subjects did you excel in (or enjoy the most) at school, college, or university?

What would you consider your natural talents, skills, and abilities to be?

What are your current interests and hobbies?

Are there any causes, groups, or clubs that you regularly participate in or support?

What subject or skill would you like to learn more about?

What do you enjoy most about the work you do now?

What is one thing you just *love* to do?

What are you most passionate about?

What image of yourself do you hope you project?

Write down your favorite quote and explain why it's your favorite.
Quote:

Why it's my favorite:

What was the most important lesson you learned from your mother? What did she stand for?

What was the most important lesson you learned from your father? What did he stand for?

If you took the lessons learned from both your mother and father and combined them into one statement, what would that statement read?

If you could be anybody in the world, who would you be and why?

If you had unlimited time and resources, what would you choose to do in life?

How do you think you could possibly add value either to another life or to society as a whole?

If you feel like there is a gift trying to emerge from you, how could you share it? Where could you begin? Note that your passion often leads to your gift.

I would just love to <fill in the blank>.

Chapter 8

The Nine Types of Intelligence

According to Howard Gardner, professor of cognition and education at the Harvard Graduate School of Education, our intelligence should be measured beyond the narrow scope of the classic intelligence quotient (IQ) test or the verbal-linguistic and logical-mathematical skills primarily used for evaluating students in school.

After more than twenty years of research, Gardner has identified at least seven other types of intelligence, which can explain why amazing, gifted students often go unnoticed by the school system or are incorrectly labeled because they are being narrowly tested on only two of the possible nine types of intelligence. Most of us possess a unique mix of these intelligences, with some types being more prominent than others. As you read the following descriptions, give yourself a score from 1 to 10, as you discover where some of your additional talents may lie.

Verbal-Linguistic Intelligence
Very good with spoken and written language. Possess a wide vocabulary. Enjoys reading, writing, telling stories, and doing crosswords. Writers, editors, public speakers, and politicians draw on this type of intelligence.

My score: 1 2 3 4 5 6 7 8 9 10

Logical-Mathematical Intelligence
Strong in both math and logic. Good at problem-solving and reasoning. Computer programmers, researchers, scientists, engineers, detectives, and accountants draw on this type of intelligence.

My score: 1 2 3 4 5 6 7 8 9 10

Visual-Spatial Intelligence
Good at visualizing and mentally manipulating objects. Often artistically inclined, has a strong visual memory, and is proficient at solving puzzles. Graphic designers, artists, photographers, interior designers, sculptors, and engineers draw on this type of intelligence.

My score: 1 2 3 4 5 6 7 8 9 10

Bodily-Kinesthetic Intelligence
Skillful at using hands or body. Express themselves through movement. Great motor skills, a good sense of balance, and expert hand-eye coordination. Athletes, dancers, builders,

actors, firefighters, mechanics, craftspeople, and surgeons draw on this type of intelligence.

My score: 1 2 3 4 5 6 7 8 9 10

Musical Intelligence
Good with music and hearing. Sensitive to sounds, tones, rhythms, and pitch. Musicians, composers, producers, singers, songwriters, audio engineers, DJs, and dancers draw on this type of intelligence.

My score: 1 2 3 4 5 6 7 8 9 10

Social-Interpersonal Intelligence
Uncanny ability to relate to and understand others. Good at communicating and sensitive to others' moods, feelings, intentions, temperaments, and motivations. Tend to be extroverted. Counselors, salespeople, politicians, business leaders, managers, and teachers draw on this type of intelligence.

My score: 1 2 3 4 5 6 7 8 9 10

Spiritual-Intrapersonal Intelligence
Thorough understanding of one's emotions, inner feelings, values, dreams, and personal philosophy. Often characterized as being "in their own world." Tend to be introverts. Writers, philosophers, gurus, psychologists, and inventors draw on this type of intelligence.

My score: 1 2 3 4 5 6 7 8 9 10

Naturalist Intelligence
Sensitive to—and appreciative of—nature. Possess highly developed levels of sensory perception and are keenly aware of their surroundings and changes in the environment. Gifted at nurturing and growing things. Conservationists, gardeners, farmers, veterinarians, marine biologists, and astronomers draw on this type of intelligence.

My score: 1 2 3 4 5 6 7 8 9 10

Existential Intelligence
Sensitive to (and having the capacity to tackle) deep philosophical questions about human existence, such as the meaning of life, consciousness, life after death, and whether life exists on other planets. Philosophers, theologians, psychiatrists, psychologists, social workers, counselors, and life coaches draw on this type of intelligence.

My score: 1 2 3 4 5 6 7 8 9 10

Use the space below to list all the intelligences for which you scored 7 or above.

Chapter 9

Your Statement of Purpose

> The heart of human excellence often begins to beat when you discover a pursuit that absorbs you, frees you, challenges you, or gives you a sense of meaning, joy, or passion.
> ~ Terry Orlick

Have you ever been to a circus and noticed that the elephant is restrained by a rather thin rope tied to its ankle? A young elephant's initial training begins with it being harnessed to a strong chain held firmly in place by a large stake driven deeply into the ground. Every time the elephant pulls, it immediately feels the resistance in the chain that defines its perimeter and demarcates just how far it can go. Gradually, the chain is exchanged for thinner and thinner ropes, and the elephant stops pulling every time it feels the tension of the rope. With the memory of the old chain firmly embedded in its mind, the elephant never realizes that it could easily pull away and take the whole tent along with it, if it chose.

The *only* limitation that exists is in the elephant's mind. It no longer tries to pull away because it *believes* it can't. That belief then defines its reality. Now it's time for *you* to remove the "chains" and self-imposed boundaries that have been holding you back. If you don't make a conscious effort to visualize and somewhat plan your future, then you run the risk of your life being shaped entirely by your environment, circumstances, or other people's values, opinions, and beliefs.

> **Accept no one's definition of your life—define yourself.**
> ~ Harvey Fierstein

Your statement of purpose will be a summary of the information gathered from the previous two chapters, with you getting totally creative and being confident enough to choose exactly what you would like to have in your life. You must know what you want before you can get it. Your life purpose comes from inside you; there is nothing external that can tell you what it is, so listen to your inner voice and let it guide you. This is where you really begin to dream.

> **Listen to the whisper before it becomes a scream.**
> ~ Oprah Winfrey

Chapter 9: Your Statement of Purpose | 63

If you will, imagine for a moment that two of you exist. There's the you that's here right now reading this, and then there's the you that you envision in your mind. Imagine that the version you see in your mind, actually exists as a template for who you could be—where all you have to do is act like the vision you see in your mind until it eventually becomes your reality. You were blessed with an imagination so that you might transcend this physical world, but it's up to you to give this version of yourself (the one you see in your mind) permission to actually exist in the real world as we know it.

> **It takes the same amount of effort whether you dream big, dream small, or not dream at all. Why not dream big?**
> ~ Bobby Minor

Your statement of purpose will help you identify your reason for being—answering questions like these:

- Who am I?
- What do I stand for?
- What do I do?
- Why do I do it?
- How does it make me feel?
- How does it make others feel?
- What do I ultimately want to accomplish with my life?

Deep in your heart, it's the thing you know you were born to do. You've felt it and seen it. It's the vision that occasionally flashes across your mind before that little voice says, "Who, you? Pleeease, get real." And then you proceed to push it as far out of your mind as possible as you quickly return to the "busyness" of life.

> **It is our light, not our darkness, that most frightens us. We ask ourselves, who am I to be brilliant, gorgeous, talented, fabulous? Actually, who are you not to be?**
> ~ Marianne Williamson

If all of us actually listened to that little voice (the voice that consequently keeps us "little"), what would life be like today? There would be no entertainers, athletes, entrepreneurs, scientists, or pioneers. Come to think of it, there would be no computers, electricity, cars, books, internet, WiFi, or any other breakthrough invention you can think of. It's the visionaries who make all these things possible and continue to push life forward by having the courage to follow their dreams—why shouldn't you be one of them?

Thoughts do become things! Look around you right now. Everything you see—and I mean everything other than what's created by mother nature—began as a thought in someone's mind. Therein lies the power of a thought, so use your unlimited imagination to really dream big. This exercise will be totally pointless if you don't. You live in an unlimited, totally abundant universe, so why choose to live your life with limits? What would you do if you knew there was no possibility of "failure"? (A word we will redefine in the next section.)

Imagine driving in a car with no directions and no planned destination. How long do you think you could drive aimlessly around? You're right—until the gas ran out or your car broke down. And that's exactly what can happen in your life if you are not true to yourself and your dreams.

Use this exercise to create a guiding light that will motivate and inspire you to take the steps you need to create a life that you love. This light will become the basis on which you make all life decisions, always choosing that which brings you closer to achieving your purpose. You will see how much easier the whole decision-making process becomes when you follow this simple rule. Life is calling, will you answer the call?

> **Your heart knows your true purpose.**
> **It keeps no secrets from you.**
> **All you have to do is listen.**
> ~ Dr. Robert Holden

For those who feel they may have more than one life purpose or who are multi-talented, have many interests, and just can't seem to decide on a particular path or direction, know that there is no right or wrong in whatever you choose. *You* are the ultimate creator of your reality. There is no predefined script for your life. This is your story to write, so choose the one that makes the most sense, the one you have the most ability and capacity to act upon at this moment—the one that brings the most excitement, motivation, and joy. If you carefully think about them all, only one will truly satisfy that criterion.

Indecision is the worst-case scenario, as that's the way you will continue to remain stagnant, so decide to take action in one direction or another and simply follow through without hesitation, or expectation. Your purpose will not be set in stone for the rest of your life; it's malleable and will more than likely evolve over time, but selecting a particular path right now means that you can at least begin your journey. So go ahead and make that decision one way or the other.

> **Take the first step in faith. You don't
> have to see the whole staircase,
> just take the first step.**
> ~ Martin Luther King, Jr.

Using all of the knowledge gathered in this section, answer the following questions:

1. What is my purpose?

Chapter 9: Your Statement of Purpose

> **You are the only one you will ever have.**
> **You have everything you need inside of you.**
> ~ Jackie Cornelius

2. How can I make a difference in the world? (What group of people do you think you could inspire? In what ways could you help them succeed? Is there a way that people could learn from your mistakes? If you offered a product or service, what would it look like? Is anybody out there already doing something close to what you're thinking about? If so, could you possibly partner with any of these services in a way that would allow you to fulfill your purpose?)

3. What life experiences have prepared me for this purpose?

Part III

Laying the Foundation

Chapter 10
Foundation Basics 101

Now that you've decided on your purpose, here are a few tips to help you create the foundation that will be necessary for creating a life you love.

<u>Monitor Your Thoughts</u>

First things first: you will consciously need to cut down on the negative, self-critical thoughts your mind is so used to generating. I once called a friend to ask for directions, and when she couldn't help me she immediately said, "Oh, I'm so useless, I can't even give you directions." I hastily replied, "No, you're not useless, you just don't know where that particular location is, no big thing!" Her language indicated to me that she was so used to thinking negative thoughts about herself that she even saw her inability to give directions—not even in general, but in this one instance—as evidence of her own worthlessness.

How often do we tear ourselves down with similar thoughts: I never get it right, I'm so fat I just can't lose weight, I'm hopeless, what's wrong with me? Give yourself a break! If we had friends who talked to us the way we talk to ourselves, I doubt they would remain friends for long. *Never* speak of yourself in a critical, disempowering manner, even in jest. Pay attention to the thoughts and feelings you have throughout the day. A single negative thought that starts out like a drip of water can gain enough momentum to become a flood if you allow it—and yes, the same applies for positive thoughts too.

Good thoughts bring forth good fruit, and bad thoughts produce rotten fruit. One constructive thought pulverizes a negative one, so the simplest thing to do is whenever you find yourself indulging in a negative thought or feeling, simply replace it with a positive one. The only way not to think about something is to immediately think about something else.

Consciously change your weak, pessimistic thoughts to positive ones until your mind realizes that those discouraging thoughts are no longer acceptable and that you refuse to participate in that kind of internal dialogue. You will never be able to erase negative thinking altogether, but with practice your mind will eventually become accustomed to automatically producing more optimistic and productive thoughts.

Let Go of Past Hurts and Disappointments

One of the hardest things to do in life is to let go of past hurts and disappointments. Being unable to let go of these experiences is a sign of unexpressed, repressed feelings. Not knowing how to deal with the pain, you chose not to deal with it at all. But if you don't allow yourself to feel (and deal) with the pain, then there is no way to escape the hold these events have over you. Eventually, you will become angry, sad, resentful, cynical, and bitter—and who wants to be there?

Besides, living in the past limits your ability to fully live in the present. The past is what it is—merely a situation over which you no longer have any power or control. So why dwell on it now? It's over. Done. Kaput. The only outcome you can determine is what you are going to do with your life right now, in the present, here, today.

> **Past experiences should be a guidepost, not a hitching post.**
> ~ D. W. Williams

Change your perspective on pain and realize that it is actually just a catalyst for change. Look at some of your past hurts: What did you learn from them? Would you have learned those lessons any other way? After the initial shock, didn't they bring about a beneficial change in your life or behavior? How are you using those experiences positively in your life today? Think about it. What will you no longer accept in the future?

I have always said that we only have two reasons for living, and they are to love and to grow. So let's deal with both of these right now. In order to keep loving and growing, you've got to heal so you can move forward and enable yourself to live your life fully and not just on "mute." A huge part of healing is forgiving. Forgiveness loosens the grip of past hurts and enables you to enjoy the positive things that exist in your life today—and believe me, there are plenty of them.

Sometimes the person you need to forgive is yourself. If you're wallowing in regret over past mistakes, know that you did the best you could with what you had at the time. You have to know that. Okay, maybe in retrospect you could have done things a little differently, but without the experience and knowledge that you gained from the situation, you had no way to know what other actions you could have performed.

Research has shown that the act of writing down feelings speeds up the healing process. Revealing pent-up, unacknowledged feelings forces you to bring them to the surface where they can be finally acknowledged and released. Don't expect this to be easy. A friend who carried out this exercise could not believe the anger, tears, and frustration she experienced during the process. But she did say that as soon as it was over she immediately felt a sense of relief, as if a huge burden had been lifted from her. My hope is that the same will happen for you.

The Exercise

1. Identify an event, experience, or person that caused you pain in the past.

2. If it was an event or an experience, relive the situation in order to fully describe it. How did it make you feel? Why did it hurt you? How do you feel about it today? How does it still affect you? Write it all down.
3. If it was a person (including yourself), do the same. What did they do that hurt you so badly? What were the consequences of their actions? How does it still affect you today? Why is it so hard to let go of those feelings? What are you scared of now? Relive the experience and feel all the pain associated with it as you write everything down.
4. When you are finished, add the following words to the end: "I forgive and release (the event or person's name) both mentally and spiritually. I now understand that this event occurred in order for me to reach my highest good because I am so loved and supported. I release all hurt and anger associated with this situation, and now choose to set myself free."
5. Read everything you just wrote and allow yourself to really feel the emotions.
6. Once you are done, rip the paper to shreds. Burn it, bury it, whatever. Just get rid of it. This action reinforces your wish to be completely done with the issue. So now be done with it.
7. Take a few deep breaths.
8. Smile. Even when you fake a smile, the movement of the facial muscles causes the release of dopamine and serotonin in the brain, which generates feelings of happiness. So it's totally fine to fake it before you make it! Smiling also stops distressing emotions, because you can't feel anxious, angry, or sad while you're smiling.

> **Sometimes your joy is the source of your smile, but sometimes your smile can be the source of your joy.**
> ~ Thich Nhat Hanh

Get Rid of Toxic People

Who or what is a toxic person? You know very well! He or she is that person you talk to that leaves you feeling utterly drained, depressed, or unmotivated once the conversation is over. This is not just something that happens occasionally; you end up feeling this way after almost every conversation with this person. Truth be told, you don't particularly like this Debbie Downer or Donald Drag, but for some reason—maybe out of pity, guilt, or sheer boredom—you chose to occasionally engage with them.

Their conversations are usually drenched in negativity. They are often bitter, angry, and resentful, and are always the victim of some unpleasant situation. Toxic people spend the entire conversation blaming, complaining, and just straight bitching. The exchange always revolves around them—their issues, their problems, just me, me, me. Although you try to offer solutions, they can't seem to hear you—hence the draining. These people revel in their own misery—and misery loves company, which is exactly why they're manipulating you into a drawn-out, depressing conversation about them.

Does this situation sound familiar? How do you get this negative energy out of your space? Short of changing your phone number, quitting your job, moving away, or leaving the country (which is what I had to do, lol), you have to do whatever it takes to avoid contact. Although you can't do anything to modify their behavior, you can definitely do something about yours. It's important to zealously guard your energy and emotional well-being, so take charge. Limit the amount of time you spend talking to this person, and find effective ways to quickly end the exchange ("I'm busy right now," "I have to go, something's on the fire that's about to burn").

Be careful not to become confrontational with these individuals—they love getting a rise out of people and (supposedly innocently) ruffling feathers. Always remain calm and detached—do not give them any of your energy. Self-preservation is key. There's a reason why you end up feeling totally drained after talking to them—the exchange is simply a transfer of energy in which you take on their negative vibes and they "steal" your positive ones. Therefore, just don't participate. I'm not being mean, but unless you're medically qualified to deal with this type of individual there's very little you can do to help their situation. Plus, that isn't their goal anyway.

Find Your Cheerleaders

Your cheerleaders are the people you go to for support, understanding, comfort, and, most of all, inspiration. Genuine, open-minded, and honest, these people provide sound advice and can always find the silver lining in any dark cloud you present. Conversations with them uplift your spirit and put that familiar smile back on your face.

As you embark on this journey of self-exploration, introspection, and expansion, it will be important to surround yourself with these positive, supportive, motivated individuals who can easily get you back on track and cheer you on when necessary.

> **You deserve to have wonderful, supportive and loving people in your life. In fact, life is too short to spend time with people who don't help you be your best self.**
> ~ Vanessa Van Edwards

It will also be important to surround yourself with positive materials, like books, DVDs, music, or audio books. Attend lectures, seminars, and workshops where you can meet like-minded individuals. Use anything that helps you stay in a positive frame of mind. See the "Resources" section at the back of the book for my list of suggestions. And just so you know, I have read every single book listed back there over the years—and have also used the presented meditations. I wouldn't recommend anything I haven't actually tried and tested myself.

Chapter 11
Foundation Basics 102

<u>Eliminate Worry and Fear</u>

Worry: To torment oneself with disturbing thoughts.

Fear: A distressing emotion aroused by impending danger, evil, pain, etc., whether the threat is real or imagined.

The worries and fears we will discuss here are the delusions we have, where no real harm or threat exists. I am still trying to understand whether worry creates fear or if it is fear that creates worry. The matter is up for debate. When I look at both definitions, however, it is obvious to me that these feelings are created in the mind and come from how we choose to *think* about things and not necessarily from those things themselves.

We worry about everything—our future, the economy, our jobs, the kids, money, bills, debt, our health, dying, being alone, crime, terrorism, war—you name it. We are so accustomed to worrying that we almost feel guilty for feeling good for an extended period of time. If we're lucky enough for that to happen, then we wait and almost expect something bad to be lurking around the corner. We are even afraid to let people know how we feel. To the question of "How are you?" the response is often, "Oh, I'm not doing too bad." Bad? What's wrong with good? I'm good! I'm great! I'm perfect! The next time someone asks you how you're doing, say in a high-pitched voice, "I'm perfect!" and then please send me an email describing the look you received.

The trick that worry plays on us is that these types of thoughts are biased. We find things to worry about all the time, but why don't we flip the coin and realize that no matter what comes our way, we will have (or find) the necessary tools to deal with it at that time? Situations always adjust themselves over time. Just look at your past to prove that statement true.

What's the point of fretting over troubles that may or may not arise? It's estimated that 85 percent of what we worry about never happens anyway, so what a waste of brainpower! The future doesn't exist anywhere but in your mind, so all these future events that you're worrying about technically don't even exist. Why not just wait until whatever it is actually happens, before you start worrying about it? But worrying is a habit. Besides that, you ingest materials daily in the form of newspapers and newscasts that back up and reinforce every worry you have—they probably add a few more items to your daily worry list too. Here are a few simple tips that can help you deal with worrisome thoughts whenever they arise:

1. Go on a media fast for about a week—and yes, this includes…wait for it…*all* social media. No newspapers, no news, no depressing stories; we are just going to quit this addiction cold turkey. After a week, see how you feel and whether you find yourself worrying as much. If you can keep this negativity fast going, then please do so, but if not, at least make sure you limit the amount of negative media you take in. Find comedies and pleasant, uplifting shows to watch, or "happy" stories to read instead.

2. Every time a worrying thought arises, zap it with an affirmation or hit it with the exact opposite thought.

    Negative: I may lose my job.
    Positive: I'll find another one; there are a trillion jobs out there. With all my experience, I'll probably make an even better salary than before.

    Negative: My car might break down.
    Positive: I'll rent one, hitch a ride with my colleagues, or take public transport. That will be fun, I haven't done that in a long while.

3. When a worrying thought arises, focus for a few minutes on something that is right in front of you, in order to practice being in the now. Use all of your senses: look,

listen, touch, smell, or taste. Really take in the subject at hand as if you are about to compose a detailed essay about it. Although that worry might pop back into your mind, do this step a few times to let your mind know you are taking control of what and how it thinks. Don't let up!

4. Another idea is to keep a "worry pad." Every time a worry arises, simply write it down on the pad with the intention of going back and worrying about it later. Then forget about it. Although this technique may sound preposterous, it works, because it allows you to express your worry and get it out of your system. It is done in a way that allows you to cultivate the habit of postponing worry, thereby reconditioning the mind not to dwell on worries in the present. See, there is a method to my madness!

There's No Such Thing as Failure

Is there some past event or occurrence that you can't seem to let go of because you consider yourself to be a failure in it? Is there something you're holding onto that is currently robbing you of being happy in the present? Well, I've got news for you, the new definition of failure is "feedback." I am completely erasing the word "failure" from the dictionary (well, in my mind anyway) and replacing it with the word "feedback," where feedback is defined as information that comes in the form of a learning experience that provides a basis for improvement.

Let me you give an example. Four millionaires under the age of thirty-five once appeared on *The David Susskind Show*. The question asked of each was how many different careers or businesses they had been in before reaching the one that allowed them to be officially classified as a millionaire. Come to find out, they had worked in an average of seventeen businesses before reaching the one that gave them millionaire status. My question then is, did they *fail* in seventeen different careers and businesses, or were these simply lessons and feedback provided to teach them what they needed to know in order to become millionaires in the future?

> **Never place a period
> where God has placed a comma.**
> ~ Gracie Allen

Would you consider Abraham Lincoln, Thomas Edison, the Beatles, or Colonel Sanders as being failures? Abraham Lincoln had three failed businesses and seven failed political campaigns before he finally became president of the United States. Thomas Edison's teachers labeled him as being "too stupid to learn anything." Yes, Edison, the very same prolific inventor who ended up holding 1,093 US patents and who we all know is credited with inventing the light bulb. The chart-topping Beatles were initially rejected by Decca Studios, who said, "They have no future in show business." And then there's our beloved Colonel Sanders. The man's chicken recipe was rejected by 1,009 establishments before he finally heard a "yes" for his now world-famous Kentucky Fried Chicken.

How many of us, if we were Colonel Sanders, would have given up and retired to being a failure after the hundredth rejection? Would you even have reached *that* far? So before you sign yourself off as being a failure, or allow somebody else to define you as one, change your perspective and realize that these situations are simply feedback and clues about something you may need to do differently in the future. Don't waste the experience. You determine whether it is going to affect you negatively or positively—that's how much in control you are. *You* determine the ultimate outcome.

Take Responsibility for Your Life

Now is the time to step up to the plate and take full responsibility for your life. How long can you go on blaming others and making excuses for the things *you* need to put right in your life? You can't expect others to pick up the slack for you, you've got to be 100 percent responsible for yourself—and aren't you worth it? Taking on a victim mentality disempowers you and leaves you feeling helpless and bitter.

Taking responsibility is the starting point of true growth. When you see yourself consistently taking action and helping yourself, you will realize your ability to make significant choices and changes, and as a result, you will reclaim your personal power and self-esteem. Those who have a sense of control over their lives are happier, healthier, and as a result more likely to achieve the levels of success they desire.

Clear the Clutter

> **If you have a pile of papers in your room, your energy automatically dips because you know it needs attention. Every time you walk into your home and there are things that need repairing, junk that needs cleaning, your energy can't flow internally because of what is happening externally.**
> ~ Karen Kingston

Karen Kingston's statement says it all. As you clear your mind, reduce noise, and come to a place of inner peace, you need to create an environment that supports the flow of positive energy into your life. Reduce spatial noise by throwing out or organizing old letters, junk mail, receipts, files, magazines, newspapers, checkbooks, bank statements, clothes, and other items you may have lying around your house. Go through each room, cleaning and clearing. In case you need help, or have ever been accused of being a pack rat, the rule for throwing out is if you haven't used it in a year then it's got to go!

When I emigrated to the Caribbean many years back, I had to pack a three bedroom, two-story house into a sum total of three large suitcases. At first it was terribly difficult to let go of my belongings but the more I cleared the easier it got, until I felt totally liberated and realized how much "stuff" I had that was just not that necessary in my life.

Having considered myself a minimalist, I was quite shocked by the revelation. After the experience I told a friend that I wanted to either live a life where I would never need any of it again or have them replaced with items I would consider to be ten times better. Either one sounded good to me.

    I urge you to get rid of the old, stale, stuck energy that surrounds you in order to make space for something new. So why are you still reading? I believe you've got work to do!

Chapter 12

Controlling the Theater in Your Mind

It is estimated that we process around sixty thousand thoughts a day. That's a ton of thinking, right? How many of these thoughts do you think are productive? How many do you think we consciously create? The mind is so out of control that it says absolutely anything, anytime, all the time—and statistics show that over 80 percent of the thoughts we think are actually negative and pessimistic. Our minds not only have to be tamed but also trained into thinking more positive, empowering, constructive thoughts—as opposed to the negative, doubtful, self-sabotaging thoughts they are so accustomed to generating.

As you begin some of the exercises presented in the next section, you can expect this theater in your mind to really put on a performance. It has been running the show up until now, and it's not going to enjoy relinquishing control as you come in and take over the production. You'll hear it say things like, "Aw, c'mon, this is a waste of time, we could actually be doing something fun right now," or "Ohhh, *How to Get Away with Murder* is about to start, let's put this off until tomorrow when we'll have more time," or "This again! Are you losing your mind with this rubbish? You need to get real about your life."

To avoid being disciplined, this little trickster will say just about anything to deter you from your reprogramming activities. You have to take control and persevere in order to get the results you want. A magnetized piece of iron will lift twelve times its weight, but demagnetized it will not even lift a paper clip—you'd better believe we are about to get magnetized!

An unexercised mind will slowly decline to minimal, boring, repetitive actions, which is possibly why you have not achieved some of the things you would have liked. You know what it takes to get your body in shape and your mind will require the same type of regular, rigorous training. You can't expect to visit the gym a couple of times and come out with the perfect body—we'd all be in great shape if that were the case. It takes dedication and commitment to see the results you would like in your body, and it will take the same type of dedication to change your thoughts to the point where you can see some of the results you would like in your life.

The main objective of part IV of this book is to give you tools that will help you feel different at your core. Remember what we learned about vibration: it is not your circumstances that determine your state of being, it is the other way around. Your state of being determines your circumstances. Now, please read that sentence again, very slowly and very carefully.

At the end of the day, the only thing you have complete control over is how you feel (or your vibration). You can't wait for a condition to change before allowing yourself to feel good, because you cannot feel (good) in the future, you can only feel in the now, and if you learn to feel good in the now then the manifestation of what you want almost becomes irrelevant, since you have already experienced it in vibration.

For instance, if there's an issue with your finances that's really getting you down and you think that having more money will bring you peace of mind, then attempt to start acting more peacefully now—right here, right now. Act as if the state of your finances has improved and already brought the peace you would expect. Get that particular "well-being" vibration going on. That's ultimately what will make you more abundant—living and acting as if <whatever it is…fill in the blank here> has already happened. You have to change how you feel on the inside so that your outside can reflect your internal change. And the only way you can change the way you *feel* is by changing your thoughts.

Think of your life as a mirror. If you go to a mirror with a frown on your face, then that's what you will see reflected back. The reflection (of your life) is not going to change externally until *you* change internally. Once *you* smile, the reflection in the mirror *has to* change and mirror that smile. It's almost as if we have to practice a certain vibration over a period of time before we can see the result in the form of a manifestation.

> **Life is a mirror and will reflect back to the thinker what he thinks into it.**
> ~ Ernest Holmes

Imagine a doctor who is about to perform surgery without a lick of prior training. What do you think will happen to the poor patient he operates on? Just as a doctor has to be adequately trained before he can perform an operation, you must train your vibration and prepare it for the manifestations of your desires. The very first step in doing that will be making peace with where you are right now, so you can drop all resistance going forward. And after all, when you think about it, where you are right now is perfectly fine because it just happens to be the beginning of where you're about to go next. I love that fact! (And hope you come to love it, too.)

Chapter 13

How We Learn

I recommend a daily routine that starts out with a maximum of two (or possibly three) of the methods presented in the next section. I think it's important to get into a basic routine with a few of the exercises first. If you try too many at once, you may possibly end up bailing early, without seeing the results you'd like. You have to ease "the theater in your mind" into this gently—almost in a coaxing fashion.

Just like when you go to the gym, you should start with the light weights before moving on to heavier equipment (or in our case, adding more processes to your routine). The methods will help to create and strengthen new neural pathways that will eventually sink down into your subconscious and take shape as new beliefs, while your old negative thought patterns eventually lose their grip as you no longer supply them with the energy and focus they need to survive.

Although we learn in various ways, there are three main learning styles: visual, auditory, and kinesthetic. Most of us learn through a combination of these methods, depending on the subject at hand, but each of us has a primary learning style, as described below.

Visual learners learn by seeing things. They need to actually see or read information and benefit from visual materials such as diagrams, graphs, charts, pictures, and films. They usually have a wonderful imagination and can be quite creative. A visual learner may use phrases like "I see what you mean," "I get the picture," or "I'll look into that."

Auditory learners are much more able to remember and understand what they *hear*. They like to have facts and details vocalized in some way, preferring recorded material, reading out loud, and participating in group discussions. They may often be seen repeating facts with their eyes closed, and may use phrases like "I hear you" or "Yes, it's loud and clear."

Kinesthetic learners deal with feelings and emotions and learn best when they are either experiencing or experimenting. They learn by doing and benefit from a hands-on approach, not really understanding how something works until they actually get to use it. Taking in learning material as they walk, jog, or play music in the background can be very effective for them. They are usually good at sports, science, biology, or other exploratory types of study. They also enjoy taking field trips to museums and galleries. A kinesthetic learner may use phrases like "Ohhh, I love it" or "Let me see how it feels."

As you go through some of the reprogramming exercises coming up, make sure to pick the methods that are most conducive to your particular learning style and those that you gravitate toward the most.

Part IV

Steps to Transforming Your Life

Chapter 14

Surrender

The very first thing you need to do is surrender—where surrender is defined as yielding to the power, control, or possession of another. Sounds totally un-motivating and weak, right? And besides, who wants to be remembered as a loser? But let's examine the statement further: "Surrender is defined as yielding to the power, control, or possession of another." Another? Who or what could this "another" be? You see, surrendering is not about throwing your hands up in defeat and giving up, it just means that you've tried all you can and you're consciously choosing to let go, whatever the issue happens to be. It's actually an act of courage and not weakness. It means that you're going to *allow* things to happen as opposed to forcing them to happen. Sounds crazy, right? But if you don't move yourself out of the way, then you leave absolutely no room for a higher power to be able to work *through* you.

> **We are at our most powerful the moment
> we no longer *need* to be powerful.**
> ~ Eric Micha'el Leventhal

At the end of the day, it all boils down to the ego. Our egos are so puffed up that they think they control and are responsible for absolutely everything. Right about now your ego is so tired and overworked that it needs a serious vacation. I mean, how can you expect it to be responsible for absolutely everything that goes on in your life? But unfortunately, that's the workload you've assigned to it.

The ego was originally tasked with keeping us safe. Aware of our surroundings in case a saber-toothed tiger (or the likes) happened to be lurking around the corner, awaiting its prey somewhere in the forest. These days we just don't run into those types of dangers (well, most of us anyway). But since the ego needs to feel important and employed, it has taken on another role—one that it is not adequately trained for. You see, it's still keeping us safe, but just not in the best of ways. It's constantly talking us down in certain situations: "Oh, don't do that, you might fail," "Don't volunteer, you'll end up making yourself look stupid," or "There is no way he would go for someone like you, honey, save yourself the heartbreak."

This fragile little voice that keeps you locked away in your own *little* world is filled with nothing but anxiety, worry, and fear. This voice is so convincing that in most cases we actually believe everything it tells us, but the problem is that it's based on false identification. The ego is not *who* you are! But you have listened to it so much and for so long that now you are *allowing* it to define who you are—and that is not its job.

> **Banish the ego and develop the spirit of
> surrender. You will then experience bliss.**
> ~ Sri Sathya Sai Baba

Surrendering simply means quieting the voice of the ego (which the following chapters will help you with) and accepting that you are okay no matter what the situation looks like on the outside. It means that you stop fighting and allow for the natural flow of things to occur. It's like being in a paddle boat with the oars going at a hundred miles per hour and your arms flailing all over the place, and although you're exerting a ton of effort, you simply end up spinning in circles. Then, all of a sudden you stop rowing and discover that your paddle boat floats along with the natural flow of the river just fine without your help—you can then sit back and relax.

> **The energy of surrender accomplishes
> much more than the energy of control.**
> ~ Amy Johnson

Why do we feel the need to micromanage the universe, anyway? The same universe that keeps our earth spinning in orbit, makes the sun rise every day, and makes the stars shine at night. Do you really think you are more powerful than all of that? Come on! When you realize what you've been doing up until now, it is almost laughable.

Allow the natural flow and rhythms that are built into this universe of ours to flow more easily to you and through you. The universe wants you to be in harmony with it, and it with you—so know that true spiritual surrender is a very brave, powerful, and magical thing to do.

> **The greatness of a man's power
> is the measure of his surrender.**
> ~ William Booth

Affirmations for Consciously Surrendering in the Moment

I surrender in this moment. I let go of all resistance and open myself to the boundless opportunities that may now arise. Any limitation with regard to this situation exists only in my mind.

I am a beautiful, unconditionally loved, and supported aspect of creation.

I surrender right now so I can get out of my own way and allow all that I need to be brought to me at exactly the right time, in its most perfect form.

Every problem has a solution, and the universe knows exactly what that solution is.

When I stay calm, happy, and hopeful, answers come to me more easily.

It is going to be fun to see how this plays out. I am ready to witness the magic of the universe unfold.

Infinite intelligence leads and guides me in all ways.

Things always work out for me.

In this moment I consciously choose to give my attention to things that are life-giving and make me feel good in the now.

I have infinite patience and am directed to be in the right place at the right time.

The universe has the ability to solve my problems in ways I cannot even fathom right now.

I give thanks in advance for the peaceful resolution to this problem.

Everything (and I mean, absolutely everything) is always in divine order.

Chapter 15

Meditate

The word meditation is derived from the Latin words *meditari* (to think, to dwell upon, or to exercise the mind) and *mederi* (to heal or cure). No longer just a practice for monks, yogis, and gurus, this ancient art has now been adopted by mainstream culture as an effective way to unplug from the everyday noise of life and transcend the incessant chatter of the conscious mind. Getting into a relaxed, stress-free, peaceful state of mind is essential for producing more positive, happy, productive thoughts as opposed to the self-defeating, unproductive thoughts that so constantly plague the mind.

Once a particular state is experienced and practiced, over a period of time the brain will eventually "learn" that state and be able to produce it at will, showing that peace and happiness are not dependent on external circumstances but on the *frame of mind* we choose to adopt at the time. Research has shown that the practice of meditation contributes to an individual's physiological, psychological, and spiritual well-being. In particular, regularly accessing the meditative alpha, theta, and gamma states (as described previously in chapter 2) allows us to do all of the following:

- Achieve deep levels of relaxation
- Reduce stress hormone levels
- Relieve insomnia and experience restful sleep
- Accelerate learning
- Improve focus and concentration
- Enhance creativity
- Decrease irritability and moodiness
- Overcome depression and anxiety
- Increase energy
- Increase feelings of vitality and rejuvenation
- Increase happiness
- Boost self-confidence
- Exercise self-acceptance
- Increase emotional stability
- Improve health and overall well-being
- Decrease muscle tension and relieve associated pain
- Aid with postoperative healing

> **Meditation is not forcing your mind to be quiet; it's finding the quiet that is already there.**
> ~ Deepak Chopra

Two Simple Meditation Techniques

These two simple meditation techniques are perfect for beginners. You will need about fifteen distraction-free minutes for each. Pick the one that seems most appealing to you, and as you practice try not to focus your thoughts on anything in particular. If a thought does arise (which is to be expected) don't cling to it, just simply let it go—the important thing is not to judge whatever it is that comes up. Don't be hard on yourself when starting out, as meditation is not easy for beginners. The theater in your mind will really go to town once it has the floor; nonetheless, over time this little chatterbox will settle down, relax, and finally get with the program. But it will take time, practice, *and* patience.

Meditation Technique 1

1. Sit in a comfortable and relaxed position.
2. Close your eyes and roll them up slightly, as if you are trying to see the center of your forehead just above your eyebrows.
3. Place your hands on either side of your abdomen and focus on your breathing.
4. Slowly inhale through your nostrils and imagine yourself inhaling love, energy, peace, and all that supports you. You should feel your hands rise as your abdomen, sides, and lower back expand.
5. Slowly exhale through your mouth. Imagine yourself exhaling stress, anger, frustration, and negativity. You should

feel your abdomen, sides, and lower back contract.
6. Repeat steps 4 and 5 for fifteen to twenty minutes (or as long as you desire).

Meditation Technique 2

1. Sit or lie in a comfortable, relaxed position.
2. Close your eyes and focus on your breathing.
3. Start to breathe slowly, inhaling through your nose and exhaling through your mouth.
4. Take a few minutes to relax your mind by thinking about a picturesque place you find beautiful and peaceful. Your brain reacts to notions of size and color, so create a vibrant, bold, vivid vision of the scene. This could be a lake, an ocean, a forest, a mountain view, or a beautiful garden. Meditation experts call this "going to the quiet place" in your mind. Take a few minutes to enjoy this picture and envision it in as much detail as possible.
5. Once your mind is relaxed, turn your attention to your body. Imagine bringing your whole body into a state of total relaxation. Relax your muscles one by one, going from head to toe. Start at your head, and as you breathe in and out, think of your muscles releasing all tension. Go through the rest of your body in the same way—eyes, nose, mouth, neck, shoulders, back, arms, hands, fingers, chest, stomach, buttocks, thighs, calves, and feet.
6. When every area of your body is relaxed, quiet your thoughts and focus on your breathing. Once again, if a thought arises just let it go.

7. When you are ready to finish your session, concentrate as before on each area of your body, starting with your feet this time. As you breathe in and out, imagine breathing life or light into each part. You may want to apply some gentle movement to each area of your body as you bring it back to life.

Chanting

Chanting—my preferred method of meditation—is a spiritual practice that has been around for over 5,000 years and is used in virtually every cultural, spiritual, and religious tradition today. Chanting consists of rhythmically repeating a mantra, word, song, or prayer, either silently in the mind or sung or spoken out loud.

Sanskrit is the sacred language of ancient India. It is known as the oldest language in the world and considered to be "the language of the Gods." Mantras are therefore prayers that are created from sacred Sanskrit words, sounds, and phrases.

There's no need to convert to a religion in order to chant in Sanskrit, since Sanskrit is a language, not a religion. A *mala* necklace (or Eastern rosary) is often used during practice to keep count of the number of repetitions. The necklaces usually consist of 108 beads, as it is most typical for mantras to be repeated in sets of 108 (although other numbers can be used as well). Having a tactile object in hand makes it hard for you to get fidgety and gives your mind an additional point of focus, which should result in it doing less wandering.

Mantra citation is considered to be most effective when using sets of 108, because according to Vedic scriptures our bodies contain 108 major energy channels; therefore, chanting 108 times allows the sound vibration to fill all the energy lines in our body and balance them in a way that allows us to "tune" our body to that mantra's particular vibration. In other words, as sound is such a powerful force, the mantras create powerful vibrations in the body (and outside it) that consume vibrations of anger, jealousy, frustration, addiction, or other unhealthy habits and raise us to our highest vibrations of love, joy, and peace.

Here are some other reasons why 108 is considered to be a sacred number:

- The diameter of the sun is 108 times the diameter of the earth.
- The distance from the sun to the earth is 108 times the diameter of the sun.
- The average distance of the moon from the earth is 108 times the diameter of the moon.
- There are 54 letters in the Sanskrit alphabet, each having a masculine and a feminine property, and 54 times 2 gives us 108.
- The numbers 9 and 12 have been said to have spiritual significance in many ancient traditions—9 multiplied by 12 is 108.
- Some say the number 1 stands for God, the universe, or your own highest truth; 0 stands for emptiness and humility in spiritual practice; and 8 stands for infinity.

In addition to chanting 108 times, you will also need to perform the practice for 40 consecutive days. Why 40 days, you may ask? Well, it's because 40 is another sacred number that also has great significance in many spiritual traditions and cultures. In most ancient texts we see 40 days (or years) as the amount of time necessary to create a favorable environment for change.

The Bible itself is filled with passages that mention the number 40 as a benchmark for deep transformation. The flood that cleansed the earth lasted 40 days and 40 nights; before his temptation Jesus fasted for 40 days and 40 nights in the Judean desert; Moses spent 40 days on Mount Sinai receiving God's law; the prophet Elijah fasted for 40 days and 40 nights at Mount Horeb; and the time between Jesus' resurrection and his ascension into heaven was also 40 days. It seems that whenever God prepared someone for a purpose, the number 40 was always prevalent.

Also, in the last century psychologists have proven that any behavioral change requires approximately six weeks (40 days) to take hold. This includes breaking a bad habit or addiction, such as smoking, or starting a good habit, like regularly visiting the gym. Physically, it is also known that this six-week period allows the brain to go through all its biorhythms and cycles in order to initiate the possibility of permanent change.

For those who plan on using this method of meditation, I have included a few mantras along with their meanings to get you started. According to my personal experience, these mantras work in powerful and surprising ways, but I am sure you will have your own magical experiences with them. Choose only one mantra to chant over the 40-day period and *really* listen to its sound as you chant. The continuous repetition will (almost) lull you into a semi-hypnotic state where you eventually get to move beyond your thoughts and get to the stillness that can be found within.

Pronunciation is *crucial*, so I encourage you to type your chosen mantra into Google or YouTube so you can hear the correct pronunciation. As important as pronunciation is, I feel that it's your sincere intention to clear your mind and effect positive change around you that is even more important. Whenever I chant I always wish the same for everyone. In other words, I never chant just for myself.

If you skip a day (where a day is defined as from the time you wake up until the time you go to bed at night) then it will be necessary for you to start over, beginning at day one. It is also fine to repeat your mantra as often as you wish, for as long or short a time as you'd like, throughout your day.

A Few Mantras and Their Meanings

Ahem Prema:
I am divine love—may unconditional love fill me completely and radiate from my heart.

Ananda Hum:
To experience unlimited joy, freedom, and creativity.

Ananta Swa Bhava:
To declare yourself as being infinite, unbounded, and unending.

Kleem:
To attract love.

Lokah Samastah Sukhino Bhavantu:
May all beings be happy and free—and may my words and actions contribute to that in some way or form.

Om (or Aum):
Considered to be the greatest mantra of all, Om is the primordial sound, the source of all other sounds, and the source of all creation. Tuning into the Om vibration brings about inner peace, mental clarity, emotional freedom, and physical health which creates a harmonious, peaceful environment and a unity between humans and nature.

Om Aim Saraswatyai Namah:
For people in the creative arts who are looking for inspiration in the form of new ideas.

Om Brahma Namah:
To engage the creative power of the universe.

Om Daksham Namah:
This says my efforts achieve maximum results with minimal effort.

Om Dum Durgayei Namaha:
Provides protection from negativity.

Om Eim Hrim Klim Chamundayei Vicche Namaha:
Builds self-confidence and willpower when feeling weak, nervous, or lacking drive. This is also good for protection.

Om Eim Sawaswatyai Swaha:
For blessings in the areas of inspiration, creativity, knowledge, and the intellect—particularly in the areas of the arts and sciences.

Om Gam Ganapatayei Namaha:
For removing obstacles from your life. These can be obstacles to success, love, or whatever situation that you feel "stuck" in.

Om Gam Shrim Maha Lakshmiyei Namaha:
To attract abundance into your life. You can focus on a specific area such as money, friends, or love.

Om Gum Namah:
To align your awareness with the creative problem-solving power of nature.

Om Gum Shreem:
To align your desires with the flow and force of universal existence so that your desires can be fulfilled more effortless and easier.

Om Hiranyagarbhaya Namaha:
To heal the heart and emotions.

Om Hum Hanumate Namaha:
Prayer to be blessed with victory, success, strength, stamina, and power.

Om Karuna Namah:
To create a space of compassion and acceptance that encourages positive transformation for yourself and those around you.

Om Kleem Shum Shukraya Namah:
Om and salutations to the ruler of enjoyment, entertainment, and pleasure. To be blessed with love, delight, gratitude, contentment, and fulfillment.

Om Kshipra Prasadaya Namaha:
For an instant blessing when suddenly faced with a troublesome or difficult situation. This can be chanted for immediate help in a circumstance like losing your car keys.

Om Mani Padme Hum:
For producing a state of empowered compassion. If you want to effect change in the world then this is a great mantra for you.

Om Namo Narayanaya:
To bring unconditional love, joy, and a connection to divine light.

Om Parama Prema Rupaya Namaha:
To welcome love into your life in the form of a beloved.

Om Prani Dhana:
For letting go of constricted, conditioned feelings and behavior—and allowing the self to be unlimited, expanding in both love and compassion.

Om Radha Krishnaya Namaha:
To be blessed with a healthy relationship full of intimacy and passion.

Om Ritam Namah:
This says my actions and desires are supported by cosmic intelligence.

Om Shanti Om:
To attract peace and harmony into a difficult situation with others (e.g. a spouse, children, in-laws, or colleagues).

Om Sharavana-bhavaya Namaha:
For general good luck.

Om Shrim Mahalakshmiyei Swaha:
For attracting prosperity and abundance in a specific area of your life whether health, finances, etc.

Om Sri Rama Jaya Rama:
To transcend karma and purify the ego.

Om Sri Ramaya Namah:
For balancing the energy in your life and your body.

Ra Ma Da Sa Sa Say So Hung:
These eight sounds stimulate the life force energy within the central column of the spine to elicit healing.

Shreem:
For attracting wealth and abundance.

So Hum:
This says I am at one with the universe.

<u>Binaural Beats, the Shortcut to Meditation</u>

As we know, meditation essentially changes the brain's frequency from beta to alpha, theta, or gamma states. Experts often take years to learn deep meditation techniques, but binaural beat technology allows you to quickly and easily alter your state of consciousness without any prior training. This clinically proven form of meditation is safe and nonaddictive and may be used as often as you wish.

With binaural beat technology, stereo headphones are used to present two tones of slightly different frequencies. One frequency is played into the left ear, while the other is played into the right. The brain then takes these two frequencies and mixes them to create a third frequency, which is called a binaural beat. This is not an actual sound but an electrical signal that can only be perceived by the brain.

For example, the left ear is presented with a tone of 490 Hz and the right a tone of 500 Hz. When the tones are combined, the mind creates the third frequency of 10 Hz, which is the phase difference between the two. This frequency created by the difference is the binaural beat. The tone generated will sound either like a wave or a beat, depending on the actual frequency. If the generated tone is somewhere around 4 Hz then it will sound like a wave, and if around 20 Hz it will sound like a beat.

Binaural beat recordings allow us to bring about different states of mind, such as happiness, creativity, or relaxation. To improve their effectiveness, the beats are often mixed with music, ambient sounds, or guided instructions. You can find binaural beat generators in the various app stores or on CDs from music stores. Of course, you can just do a search on good old YouTube. You should also check the guided meditations presented in the Resources section at the back of this book.

Chapter 16

Set Your Intentions

Consciously creating your life by design (and not by default as you may have been doing up until now) means that it is important to start your day as well as you can. Have you ever woken up on the wrong side of the bed, feeling cranky—and mad that the alarm went off so soon—and then throughout the day you just couldn't seem to shake that waking-up-on-the-wrong-side-of-the-bed feeling? Well, setting an intention is enough to slow that momentum and shift that feeling in the opposite direction completely.

An intention allows for mindful living, as it forces you to be in the present moment as opposed to imagining a future long-term *goal* that has a definite measurable result. Intentions demand positive energy and are created from a place of love as opposed to fear—where you intend that events that happen throughout your day not only serve your highest good but also the highest good of others, too.

Setting your intent first thing in the morning tells your RAS what events or circumstances it needs to add to your high priority list for the day. Alerting this faithful servant to what you expect to happen allows it to find—and hey, possibly even orchestrate—those particular types of events and situations for you. Setting your intention influences both your inner and outer realities in a way that sets a chain of events into motion, whether immediately revealed to you or not.

How do you eat an elephant? One chunk at a time—and that's exactly how you should set your intentions, which is different from the way you set goals. (And no, I promise…I am not obsessed with elephants, lol.)

> **Intentions are not goals. Goals stifle us.
> Intentions set us free to be our best selves.**
> ~ Joan Hyman

Goal: I want to lose weight.
Intention: Today I am going to fill my body with fresh, nutritious foods that bring me vitality, health, and energy.

Goal: I want to earn my MBA.
Intention: Today I am going to spend an hour at the coffee shop in peace so I can study for my upcoming exam.

Example Intentions

- Today I intend that all my thoughts, words, actions, and deeds serve the highest good for myself and others too.

- I intend that I am in excellent physical, emotional, mental, and spiritual health.
- Today I intend to be aware of and follow my natural rhythms so that things can flow more easily into my life.
- I intend to drive to work safely today and not allow myself to be angered by other drivers, but instead to be courteous and kind on the road.
- Today in my meeting I plan to be a team member who listens intently and really tries to understand the issues so that I might contribute to a valuable solution.
- I intend to allow wonderful, supportive, loving people into my life and spend less time interacting with people who do not help me to be my best self.
- Today I intend to shut up my inner critic and instead of saying, "No, I can't," hear myself say, "Yes, I can!"
- Today I will do something special out of the blue to let my husband (or wife) know just how much I love and appreciate him (or her).
- Today is going to be one of the best days of my life.
- Today I want to practice being nonjudgmental and more understanding of myself and others.
- Today I want to let go of fear and try one thing that I have never done before.
- Today I intend to call my old friend and apologize about our misunderstanding so we can both make peace and move forward.
- Today I intend to gratefully acknowledge all the miracles and magic that are manifesting in my life.
- Today I want to be of benefit to others and lead by

example in the way I choose to show up in the world.
- Today I intend to come from a place of love, patience, compassion, understanding, forgiveness, and peace.

Just saying simple statements such as these first thing in the morning can change your whole vibration and set the tone for your day. Once you've said, written, or shared your intentions, it's important that you let it go—because once you've intended an outcome you *must* surrender the process to the universe. With goals you have to create a plan, but with intentions you *allow* the perfectly designed process to unfold in its own way, always choosing to believe in a friendly, supportive universe.

> **The most important decision we make is whether we believe we live in a friendly or hostile universe.**
> ~ Albert Einstein

If you need more intention-setting inspiration, look no further. This is my absolute favorite, and I promise that just by reciting this first thing in the morning you will experience a sense of peace and knowing like no other throughout your entire day. Here it is:

> In all my transactions today, I intend to come from a place of love within me, to a place of love within others; From a place of honesty in me, to a place of honesty within others;

From my integrity, to the integrity of others;

From a place of openness, to a place of openness as I respect the rights of all living things.

I intend to be gentle, kind, and forgiving.

I intend to be aware of the wonders of the universe and to greet them all with gratitude and awe.

I intend to welcome whatever flows into my life to teach me today,

And to listen to the conversation that the universe is trying to have with me.

I intend to be inspired, to have joy in both work and play.

To be grateful for all that I have in my life and for every opportunity I'm given.

I intend to use my intuition and all my other spiritual gifts in all transactions today and to help wherever I can, even if that help means standing still and doing nothing, or letting go of someone I love.

I intend that there shall be peace and harmony, and that

wherever I can make restitution, I shall have the courage and willingness to do so.

I intend to live my humanity and divinity simultaneously today and to move further along my path to enlightenment.

I rededicate my life to love, to peace, to harmony, to healing, to teaching, to my spiritual growth and to the spiritual growth of others.

~ Author Unknown

Chapter 17

Have an Attitude of Gratitude

Did you know that the most powerful phrase in any language after "I love you" is "Thank you"? Being in a state of gratitude forces you to focus on and appreciate what is good in your life, which in turn will help you attract even more things to be grateful for.

We've all had the frustrating experience of bending over backwards for an ungrateful person who, no matter how hard we tried, just could not be pleased. How likely are we to try to help this person again? We have also felt the joy of a nice thank you card or gesture that showed someone's appreciation for an act we did. How do you think the universe will respond when you regularly start saying thank you? It is important to be grateful for not only what you have in your life right now but also for what you are about to receive. Giving thanks for something as if it already exists opens the doors for you to (almost effortlessly) actually receive it.

If we take time to think about it, there are many things we need to be thankful for. In his book *Gateway to Happiness*, Rabbi Zelig Pliskin tells the story of a man who decided to spend a few minutes giving thanks for his morning coffee. As the young man thought the process over, he realized that workers in Brazil had to plant, tend, pick, roast, and grind the coffee beans before finally packing them into cartons for distribution in the United States. The shipping industry would then have to deliver the coffee to his local grocery store. Then he thought about the water he had used to make the coffee, the stove, the gas, and even the match he'd used to light the stove. Because he took his coffee with milk, there was also the dairy industry to consider. The man wrote furiously for more than half an hour as he became aware of the thousands of people (and processes) that were necessary for him to have his daily cup of coffee—something that up until that point he had taken for granted. This awareness led him to a heightened spiritual experience, and he began to give thanks daily for all who made it possible for him to even exist on the planet.

You have a lot to be thankful about on a daily basis also, from the hot shower you took this morning to the comfortable bed that you sleep in at night. I have adopted the practice of keeping a gratitude journal in which, at the end of each day, I write down at least five things I am grateful for. Within a few days of adopting this practice I noticed that my mind naturally began to seek out and find things to be grateful for (due to my new RAS programming).

For example, I visited a doctor at a local hospital. As I walked past the pain management center I immediately gave thanks that I was not suffering or in any type of pain. Later, as I waited for my prescription, I noticed a gentleman with a cast on his arm desperately trying to type out a note on his Blackberry. I immediately gave thanks that both my hands were free and without injury and that I could return to my office and continue working on my computer that afternoon. I'm certain that if I had not begun keeping a journal a few days before, these so-called ordinary events would have gone unnoticed by me.

According to Robert Emmons, Ph.D., a psychology professor and researcher at the University of California, gratitude research is beginning to suggest that feelings of thankfulness are tremendously valuable in helping people cope with daily problems, especially stress. Grateful people tend to be more optimistic, and there are studies that link optimism to a better-functioning immune system. So it looks like being in a state of gratefulness can help not only to reduce stress and keep you upbeat, but to keep you healthy as well.

When life gets hectic and you begin to feel overwhelmed, I urge you to take a few moments and find—right there and then—at least five things you can be grateful for. Happiness comes when you shift your focus away from the troubles you have and give thanks for the troubles that you don't.

> **Let us rise up and be thankful, for if we didn't learn a lot today, at least we learned a little, and if we didn't learn a little, at least we didn't get sick, and if we got sick, at least we didn't die; so, let us all be thankful.**
> ~ Buddha

Chapter 18

Affirm

Most of us think of affirmations as being short, simple statements such as "All is well in my world," "I love, respect, and appreciate myself," "Money flows to me effortlessly and abundantly," and so forth. What we are about to create, however, is an affirmation blueprint—or movie script, if you will—for your life. Your script should address the most important areas of your life including, but not limited to, the following:

- Your newly defined statement of purpose taken from your work in chapter 9
- The contribution you plan to make to society
- Home environment
- Family life
- Relationships
- The type of friends you would like to have
- Social life (fun and recreation)

- Career and work environment
- The type of associates, customers, or clients you would like to have
- Finances
- Health
- Desires
- General goals
- Personal development goals
- Spiritual growth goals

This is the part where you completely eliminate words like can't, try, maybe, never, suppose, might, probably, but, if, scared, impossible, and worried from your vocabulary. Look at them all—they sound disempowering and depressing. Imagine what your life would be like if these words didn't exist in the English language. Well, that's exactly what you're about to create with your script: your life *minus* these types of words.

Visualizing the life you desire will become a source of motivation and inspiration you can use often in the attainment of your life's goals. Just think about what you want, why you want it, and how having it would make you feel. Usually you want something because you think you will *feel* better from having it; so if you really think about it, all you're looking for is a *feeling*—not necessarily a "thing."

> **Feelings are the language of the soul.**
> ~ Neale Donald Walsch

When creating your affirmation script, forget completely about how, when, or if it will happen—leave these details to the all-powerful universe. Focus on everything that *could* be possible, form the image in your mind, and write it all down. Take your time to go back and edit, alter, or refine your script as necessary. Your script will allow you to stop looking at what is and instead focus on what could be. If you keep focusing on what is, then you run the risk of creating a Groundhog Day type scenario in your life. If you want things to change, then your thoughts *have to* change first. It cannot happen any other way.

It took me a couple of days to complete my script. Luckily for me, I had already been writing down positive statements, as well as taking notes from all the books I've read over the years. So creating my script involved setting a vision, including the inspirational words and phrases I had previously collected, and putting it all down on paper.

I will never forget the first day that I recited my script—it was amazing. That day I noticed how so many people randomly greeted and spoke to me on the street. A Russian gentleman even serenaded me, looking deep into my eyes as I sat outside a cafe enjoying a coffee with a friend. Although I didn't understand a word of what he sang, I was still flattered (but thought I'd better go home right away and change that part of my script to specify an English-speaking gentleman). All jokes aside, I recognized the power of the words I had created and recited for the first time that day.

At the time, I had absolutely no idea I would be writing this book and sharing my experiences and knowledge with you. A paragraph in my affirmation read as follows: "I am blessed enough to own a business that is an extension of me and an expression of my purpose here on this earth. It is very successful and serves millions of people around the world. I get to feel fulfilled and accomplished, according to my desires and values, and my sales are improving every day. It is the most exciting expression of myself I can imagine. I watch myself advance, progress, and become wealthier every single day. The more I receive the more I am able to give to others and do good on this earth."

As you can see, I had no idea how my desires would manifest at the time. But I knew exactly what I wanted, why I wanted it, and how it would make me feel. Since beginning my daily affirmation ritual I have been presented with numerous ideas for ways to fulfill my desires. Trust me, this book is just the beginning.

<u>Tips and Guidelines for Creating Your Script</u>

Here are tips and guidelines to be followed when creating your affirmation script:

It Should Be Stated in the Present
The universe responds to statements that describe conditions existing now, in the present. You should not attempt to affirm using phrases such as "I will," or "I would like," but instead affirm using "I am," or "I have." Feel the difference between "I will become more confident," and "Today I am confident." One statement is full of immediate power, while the other does not give a time frame or carry a sense of accomplishment.

When will you become more confident? Next week, next year, next decade? So state your affirmations in the present, in the now, as if what you're saying already exists.

It Should Be Stated in the Positive

You cannot negate a negative statement with another negative statement, so you should always affirm in the positive. For instance, instead of saying, "I'm not angry," say "I remain calm in all situations." With the first statement your subconscious simply skips over the word "not" and instead focuses on the word "angry," and you may experience yourself becoming irate more often. With the second statement your subconscious focuses on the word "calm" and can therefore more easily put you in alignment with your wish.

Let me show you this process in action. Right now I would like you to envision an image in your mind, but it should *not* be a pink elephant (Oh no, not elephants again!). So what did you just think of? This happened because your subconscious actually processes in images and it does not have images for words like "not," "don't," "never," or "won't." That's why it simply skipped over the word "not" and produced a picture of a pink elephant.

Keep this in mind as you create your affirmation. Make sure your statements and word selections effectively zoom in and focus on what you want and would like to create more of in your life, as opposed to what you don't. Note that it can be helpful to figure out some of the things you don't want first so that you can then accurately deduce what you do want—and that's what you'll end up putting into your script.

It Should Be Specific

You must know exactly what you want to create before you can receive it, and part II of this book should have helped you figure a few of those things out. It's impossible to reach a destination with vague, ambiguous directions, so be specific. Imagine ordering a burger from Burger King, and when it's served you say, "Oh no, I meant with ketchup and mayo, but no mustard, relish, onions, or tomatoes." The universe operates in exactly the same way, so you must make your intentions clear and describe them in as much vivid, rich detail as possible. Your statements should reflect the reality you want to create for yourself. The more clear and definite you make the picture, the stronger your desire will be. Statements such as "I am the best at everything I do," are way too vague and ambiguous for the universe to accurately execute. Look at the differences in the statements presented below.

Ambiguous: I am the best customer service representative.
Specific: I provide excellent customer service, always satisfying and exceeding my customers' expectations.

Ambiguous: I am the best snooker player in town.
Specific: Every single time I take a shot, the ball reaches my intended target.

It Should Not Be Too Specific

Now I'm about to slightly contradict what I just said. Although your affirmation should be very specific in parts, in other parts you need to allow enough room for your desires to manifest in ways that you cannot even conceive of right now. For instance, although you may want a mansion with twenty bedrooms, fifteen bathrooms, spiral staircases, heated marble floors, a fountain up front, and tennis courts and swimming pool out back, what you really want is a beautiful, safe, peaceful, loving environment that comfortably accommodates you and your family's needs. If you focus on a particular manifestation in way too much detail, then you run the risk of completely ignoring other possibilities—due to the functioning of your RAS—that may come your way.

<u>Making Your Affirmation Powerful</u>

We have already discussed neuroplasticity—the brain's ability to change its structure and rewire itself according to what it experiences—but what I didn't tell you is that the changes occur regardless of whether the experience is real or not. If a group of people performed a particular task and another group just *imagined* engaging in the task, both groups would respond and display activity in the exact same areas of the brain.

Medical research has proven that the brain cannot tell the difference between what's real and what's imagined. When a group of athletes were hooked up to electrodes and visualized themselves engaging in their particular sport, tests showed that exactly the same muscles fired in the exact same sequence as if they were actually physically performing the activity. So if your brain cannot tell the difference between what's real and what's imagined, then it's up to you to make your every fantasy become real (of course, in your mind first).

According to what we just learned, when you create your affirmation script you do not have to actually believe the whole thing initially. Remember, it's your limiting beliefs that have directed the behaviors that have manifested in you, creating some of your less desirable results anyway. So if your affirmation does not challenge your current belief system or make you raise an eyebrow here and there, then I doubt you're reprogramming or changing your beliefs in any way at all. On the other hand, don't make your script too far-fetched, as you don't want to set off your natural BS meter, which will ensure your affirmation does the absolute opposite of what you intend.

The good thing is that it is not possible to maintain two conflicting ideas over a long period of time, and eventually you will choose to adopt the one that is most frequently presented. That's why daily repetition is important. The action imprints the affirmation onto your subconscious until it accepts your statements as true. Your subconscious will sense a discrepancy between what it currently sees in its world and what actually exists in yours, and, with the help of your RAS, will attempt to fill this void by providing you with thoughts and ideas that will eventually allow the two to match. So plant the seeds of your desires in your mind and make the commitment to tend to them regularly.

> **A man reaps what he sows.**
> ~ Galatians 6:7

I recommend that you record any changes you notice—no matter how small—in some type of notebook or journal.

These changes will be definite indicators that your affirmation is working and providing change on some level. When I realized that some of my aspirations were coming true, this gave me the confidence to believe that others were coming true also. In fact, I felt like they were already there. Maybe this is what compelled me to continue. I could just *feel* it because I allowed myself to, without a shadow of a doubt in my mind.

> **Whoever says to this mountain, "Be taken up and cast into the sea," and does not doubt in his heart, but believes that what he says is going to happen, it will be granted him.**
> ~ Mark 11:23

Strong expectancy is an extremely powerful magnet, so it's important to believe that whatever you affirm will eventually come to pass. Initially, your level of expectancy may be quite low, and you may feel rather dubious as you continue to recite and train daily. But just as a professional athlete becomes stronger over time, your faith and level of expectation will begin to rise as you begin to witness and recognize the changes taking place in your life. Remember, this is all totally new to your mind so you can expect some resistance in the beginning. The key is not to give up to the theater in your mind but instead persevere.

At times you may find reciting your affirmation rather boring, and no matter how hard you try it may seem as if the message doesn't resonate within your soul. Don't worry, this is normal. Just continue to affirm daily. I remember once at around the thirty-day mark I just burst into tears while reciting my affirmation. It was almost like I felt something break inside me, like the barrier of mistrust had been broken down—and now the words could finally penetrate my soul (or subconscious).

Your affirmation should be recited daily and preferably out loud. Due to our various brain states (as described in chapter 2), the most effective times to recite your script are as soon as you wake up in the morning and just before you go to sleep at night. You will see results much more quickly if you are consistent, rather than just reciting periodically, so try not to skip a day. Doing it first thing in the morning sets your tone for the day, and running through your affirmation at night is of utmost importance as you will continue to affirm on the subconscious level while you sleep.

When reciting your affirmation out loud, you should be commanding but not demanding—there's a difference. Think of the way you feel when somebody comes up to you and rudely demands something from you. How do you feel about giving them whatever it is they're asking for? On the other hand, when someone approaches you with a nice smile and a pleasant demeanor, how do you feel about giving them their particular request? Remember this as you begin to affirm daily. Although you should speak with authority, be as pleasant, gentle, and loving (to yourself) as possible.

To increase the intensity of the thoughts you are sending, it is of utmost importance that you use your emotions to really *feel* the words you are affirming. Thoughts become things, but *only* if accompanied by *strong feeling*. Do you remember where you were on September 11, 2001? How about the name of the song that played for your first dance on your wedding day?

Or the events surrounding the birth of your first child? These experiences stay with us over time because they are deeply embedded in our minds due to the intensity of emotion that accompanied them. When you're reciting, get really excited about the vision you see for your new life. Live and feel the experience as if it were true and you had really accomplished everything you're imagining.

Lastly, your affirmation should not come from a place of desperation or need. If you are desperate or needy, then—if like attracts like—the universe will only send you more things to be desperate and needy about. Although you long for the things you want, try to be in a place where you could easily live quite happily without them. You have to be perfectly fine with where you are right now; remember, steps have to be taken to get where you want to be, so make peace with where you are now before attempting to move on.

In summary:
- Use your script to stretch your imagination and break through your limiting beliefs.
- Use your emotions to really *feel* the words as you affirm.
- Use your emotions to really *feel* the words as you affirm.
- Use your emotions to really *feel* the words as you affirm.
- Use your emotions to really *feel* the words as you affirm.
- Use your emotions to really *feel* the words as you affirm.
- Use your emotions to really *feel* the words as you affirm.
- Use your emotions to really *feel* the words as you affirm.
- Use your emotions to really *feel* the words as you affirm.
- Use your emotions to really *feel* the words as you affirm.

- Use a notebook or journal to record any changes that take place over time.
- Strong expectancy speeds up the manifestation process.
- Recite daily, preferably first thing in the morning and (or) last thing at night.
- Be commanding but not demanding.
- Do not come from a place of desperation or need.
- Persevere…the outcome will be well worth the effort!

<u>A Sample Script</u>

This day and every day, I grant myself permission to be a powerful, magnificent, creative genius. I am here to be of service and I shall use my God-given talents to do so. As I live in an abundant universe there is no limit to what I can create. The things I do and create are even better than I could ever imagine.

I know and trust that the infinite intelligence who gave me my desires will lead, guide, and reveal the perfect plan for their unfolding. I constantly attract the right people, resources, and circumstances to help me fulfill my life's mission.

I forgive and release anybody and everybody who has ever hurt me. I wish health, happiness, peace, and all the blessings of life for each and every one. I am free and they are free. It is a marvelous feeling, and I now chose to restore my heart back to love.

I love myself; therefore, I behave and think in a loving way to all people. I only attract loving people into my world for they are a mirror of what I am.

I pray to attract my soul mate who is strong, honest, peaceful, kind, loyal, and fun. He loves me for who I am and extends that love to my family. I release all fears I may have of loving someone or being loved and empower myself with the ability to both give and receive unconditional love.

My body is my temple. It effectively uses and processes all the nutrients I provide so that I remain fit and healthy. Every cell, nerve, tissue, and organ in my body is being made whole right now. I am free of "dis-ease" and I give thanks for the healing of my mind and body that is taking place right now.

My home is surrounded by peace, love, and beauty. It is a place where I am happy, comfortable, safe, and at peace. The needs of my children are always met and we grow together healthily in mind, body, and spirit each day. Love flows freely between me, my family, and those who visit us.

Money flows to me endlessly and abundantly from expected and unexpected sources. It is one of the rewards I get for adding value to the lives of others. I use it wisely, responsibly, and for good only. The more I receive, the more I am able to give and do good with on this earth. I am focused, committed, passionate, and determined in everything I do. I find joy in both work and play. I use my intuition and other spiritual gifts in all my activities. Whatever I start I bring to a successful conclusion, and all things work together for the greatest good of all.

I welcome whatever flows into my life to teach me today and give thanks for all I have as well as for the opportunities I am given.

I go forth this day relaxed, assured, confident, and in absolute peace.

Record It

Renowned Bulgarian psychologist Georgi Lozanov discovered that, while listening to certain types of music, the mind is much more receptive to new knowledge and has the ability to achieve a super-learning state. Here are a few benefits of listening to music while you learn:

- Helps you to relax
- Activates your right brain (which allows for free-flow thinking) to receive the new information
- Helps move information into the long-term memory storage banks held within your subconscious

For these reasons it will be necessary to find a relaxing instrumental music track (or binaural beat) to use as a backdrop for your recorded affirmation. Recording your affirmation in your own voice is most beneficial, as your brain knows and recognizes your voice better than anyone else's. It has also been scientifically proven that your subconscious is far more sensitive to the sound of your own voice than any other and so is far more likely to accept the affirmation and embed it permanently this way than if it were recorded in an unfamiliar, generic voice, as can be found on commercial CDs.

When recording your affirmation, speak in a calm, mellow voice. Speak at a comfortable pace that allows you to absorb the information. It should not be too fast, which can cause you to lose focus, nor should it be too slow, where your voice begins to sound unnatural. It has to be just right. If possible, aim to match your voice to the pace, tone, and feel of the music.

Having a recorded affirmation means that not only can you listen when you wake in the morning and before you go to sleep, but now you have a tool to use while engaged in your regular activities throughout the day. Whether working out, driving in your car, working on your computer, or taking a lunch break, you can affirm all day long! For this exercise you will need the following:

- A printout of your affirmation
- An MP3 instrumental backing track
- A computer (or other recording device)
- A headset that has a microphone. This is necessary so the music will not bleed out from your speakers as you record your affirmation. I recommended the Plantronics

USB stereo headset, which produces excellent, crisp, clean audio results.
- Audio recording software. For this demonstration we will use Audacity (available from <u>audacity.sourceforge.net</u>), which is a free, cross-platform sound editor.

Instructions:

1. Open Audacity.

2. Go to the File menu and select Open.

3. Navigate to your desired music file and click the Open button. A stereo waveform will appear in the window.

4. Test your microphone's input level by clicking on the Input Level Meter (or down arrow) next to the microphone icon at the top of the screen and select Start Monitoring. As you talk into the microphone you will see a red bar moving across the top. The bar should never cross the zero mark (which indicates distortion). If it does then use the Input Volume Control to turn down your mike's volume.

5. Rewind to the beginning of the track and click on the button with the red circle to begin recording.

6. Recite your affirmation. If any mistakes are made along the way, do not stop—simply recite that particular section over, right then and there. You will erase the bad parts later.

Chapter 18: Affirm | 143

7. When you're finished, click on the button with the yellow square to stop recording.

8. Immediately save the file by selecting File > Save Project.

9. Use the volume control levels (the control with the plus and minus signs on either side) for each track to create a mix that allows you to hear your voice clearly over the backing track.

10. To remove background hiss from your audio recording (remember the noise we used to get back in the day from the old-fashioned tape recorders?) mute the backing track and use your mouse to select a silent part of the vocal, either at the very beginning or at the end of the track.

11. Go to the Effect menu and choose Noise Removal. When the window appears, hit the Get Noise Profile button.

12. Go back to the Effect menu and choose Noise Removal again. When the window appears this time, hit the OK button. Play back your vocal track; just like magic, all background hiss will now be gone.

13. Use your mouse to select the entire vocal track. Select Normalize from the Effect menu. Input a value of -3.0 dB and click OK. This will even out the volume of your audio track so there are no spikes in sound (i.e., very quiet passages followed by very loud passages).

14. Experiment with the editing features of the program, using the waveform data to visually select and cut out mistakes or errors from the vocal track. Use the Zoom tool to aid with accuracy.

15. Once satisfied with your editing and mix, save the file once more by selecting File > Save Project As. This time save the file with a different name, e.g., Aff-Complete.

16. Export the file as an MP3. To do this, go to the File menu and select Export. You may need to download the LAME library from lame.sourceforge.net in order to complete this action. Just follow the prompts that are presented on-screen.

17. Now you can either burn a CD or copy the track straight into your MP3 player.

    Voila!

Chapter 19

Visualize

Now that you've created your affirmation script, what exactly does it *look* like? In part II you dug deep into exactly who you are and your reason for being, and you came up with answers that have somehow managed to elude you until now. As you see, you had the answers all along. They're not anything anybody could have given or told you, but the difference is that you took the time to explore and listen to your soul. That's the beautiful gift you have given yourself by investing in my book.

We've all heard about vision boards, which were made popular by the movie *The Secret* some time back. You may even have created a few in the past. But now, armed with the new revelations you have about yourself and what you see for your future, it's time to create a fresh, brand-new board that accurately depicts exactly what a life you love looks like.

Visualization can be extremely powerful in the attainment of your goals. If you can't visualize or picture your goals then it's unlikely you will ever achieve them. All successful men and women have used this technique throughout history, whether intentionally or not. Creating a visual representation of the things you would like to do, be, or have helps you to stay motivated as you use the tool to breathe life and energy into your dreams and as you picture your future clearly—in the now.

Your subconscious (where your beliefs are held) processes and thinks in pictures, so it's up to you to create a new story that will allow for internal change that produces external results; where you will be able to attract situations, people, and events into your life according to the "images" you choose to create and hold in your mind. The father of American psychology, William James, emphasized that the subconscious mind will bring to pass any picture that is both held within the mind *and* backed by faith. Although we've been taught (or should I say conditioned to believe) that seeing is believing, it is actually the other way around: believing is seeing. To create anything in your life, you have to create and believe it in your mind first.

> **According to your faith
> let it be done unto you.**
> ~ Matthew 9:29

That's why you never worry about the "how" of how it will happen. Worrying about the how introduces doubt and therefore contradicts the images in your mind. Simply go forward with the belief that the "how" will take care of itself and will be revealed to you once you embark on your journey.

Know that your physical mind was not created to figure out the how, or the way, that things will unfold. This is not its responsibility and is often the stumbling block we face when attempting to go in a new direction in life. "But how this… how that?" No, this is not the job of your physical mind, so do not overburden it and slow your vibration down with all that unnecessary drama. Know that your physical mind can *only* perceive the result of what has already happened. Get it? There's many a situation in your life where up until now you could not explain *how* whatever it is happened, how you made it, or how you got through it—so apply that same logic here. Make sure not to create a limiting counter-belief by trying to figure out the how.

To create your vision board, scour the internet and various magazines to find inspiring pictures, words, headlines, affirmations, acronyms, or quotes that accurately and boldly demonstrate the life you see for yourself in the future. Remember, this is all about *feeling*, so make sure the images you choose really get your feelings excited and stirred up. Don't be shy and don't be modest either! Be careful though, because, for instance, you may find a picture of a million-dollar bill, but does looking at it actually make you feel good or does it make you experience feelings of lack? There's a big difference.

If you lived the life of your dreams, what would that look like? Who would you serve? Where would you live? What kinds of places would you travel to? How would you look? What kinds of clothes would you wear? What activities would you participate in? What associations or groups would you join? What charities or organizations would you donate time and money to? What lectures or courses would you take? What lectures or courses would you give? Would you own your own business? Have you thought about a name for it, yet? If so, mock up a logo and add it to your board. Do you plan to volunteer with an existing organization? If so, add their logo to your board. Put it all down. Knock yourself out with the vision you've decided to create for your life. This is your very own personal feel-good board, and you should be able to *raise* your vibration just by looking at it.

When your board is jam-packed with images and feels complete to you, place it at eye level where it can be viewed frequently throughout the day. An office or a bedroom would be an ideal location. Make sure to view your board regularly, focusing on the pictures, the words, and the underlying theme. Emanate the feeling of it already being accomplished. How would you feel if everything on your board had been accomplished? Go with that feeling, like it's already happened, and aim to carry that feeling throughout your day.

Just in case you need some direction on how to create a vision board, here goes. You will need the following:

- Cork, poster, or foam board
- An internet connection
- A color printer (no drab uninspiring black-and-white pictures unless it particularly speaks to your theme)
- Plain or glossy (preferably glossy) printing paper
- A large assortment of magazines, pictures, catalogs, and (or) snapshots
- Glue, a glue stick, thumb tacks, tape, or blu-tack

- Scissors
- Your favorite picture of yourself (place this smack dab in the middle of your board so that your mind can get used to seeing yourself integrated into this new lifestyle)

Once it's finished, take a picture of your board. Besides hanging it up somewhere around your house or office, you can also keep a copy on your phone, tablet, computer, or any other device where it can be easily viewed to serve as a reminder and a feel-good motivational tool throughout the day.

<u>Create a Video</u>

Okay, so I have to admit that the most prized possession in my reprogramming arsenal is my affirmations movie. I love to hear the "ohhhs," "ahhhs," and "I want one of those" from the trusted friends and colleagues with whom I have shared my movie. It consists of the pictures from my dream board, selected phrases from my affirmation script, and personal acronyms that appear against the backdrop of the most beautiful music known to man (Okay, I exaggerate…but you get the picture).

Having a movie that includes text, pictures, and music helps synchronize both the left and right sides of the brain, which promotes whole-brain thinking and creativity, as well as general feelings of well-being. Every time something or someone threatens to pull me into a pool of negativity I immediately watch my movie. Within seconds there is a smile on my face, and my focus returns to exactly where it needs to be. It is truly a powerful tool!

To create your movie you will need the pictures from your dream board. They should be in either GIF or JPG format, which will not be a problem if they originally came from the internet. If you took your images from magazines and the like, then these will need to be scanned into a computer (or use your phone to take pictures of them) so they can appear in the aforementioned formats.

Organize your pictures into a logical sequence so you can pull short, simple phrases that perfectly fit what they emanate. Create a Word document of your selected acronyms and phrases so you can easily cut and paste them into the application I will describe below. Finally, select a beautiful, relaxing MP3 file to use for a musical backdrop.

Now I will share with you the real secret behind the secret, which proves this book is filled with nothing but love. Once you have all items in hand, head over to Animoto at www.animoto.com. Animoto is an online application that dares to take boring old slideshows to the next level, combining images, video, text, and music into a dynamic, original, high-quality video. Now you too can receive "ohhhs" and "ahhhs" from your trusted family and friends.

The creators of Animoto include former producers at MTV, Comedy Central, and ABC. Their application uses a patent-pending cinematic artificial intelligence technology that acts just like a movie director, using the latest and most sophisticated professional post-production techniques available in television and film today. It analyzes your selections, taking into account every nuance of your music track, in order to create a video that has incredible image transitions that sync perfectly with your backing track. It is truly spectacular! The best part is that no technical skills are required. All you have to do is follow the simple on-screen instructions to upload and arrange your text, music, and images into a complete production.

A personal account costs sixteen dollars a month, or you could opt to try the 14-day free trial of the Professional package—but hey, you didn't hear that from me (wink, wink!). Animoto will create a mix of your video, which you can put through as many "remixes" as you like. They promise that no two videos will ever be the same, and I can vouch for that. It is fun, fun, fun!

Animoto downloads are available in MP4 format, which can be played directly on your computer using QuickTime or iTunes. Importing the video into iTunes (or other) will facilitate its transfer to your iPhone if you have one. A high-resolution DVD-quality version of the video can be ordered and downloaded for an additional fee. It comes in the form of an ISO file which can be burned directly to DVD.

Chapter 20

Afform

In his book titled *The Book of Afformations*, Noah St. John advocates creating "afformations," a term he coined for a tool that helps us change our underlying thoughts and behaviors from negative to positive. St. John believes that any problem we pose in our mind takes the form of a question that is in search of an answer, so when we ask a question, our mind's automatic function is to go out and seek an answer. Common everyday questions may be: "What time is it?" "Where did I park the car?" "How much does this cost?" or "Where are you going?" We constantly ask ourselves (or someone else) questions that we expect to receive answers to. With regard to our personal lives, we may have asked questions like:

- Why am I such a failure?
- Why am I so fat?

- Why didn't I get that promotion?
- Why won't this work for me?
- Why is my wife so moody all the time?
- Why do I never have enough money?

If we are constantly asking ourselves these negative types of questions, we can expect (because of where we're putting the majority of our focus) to see and experience more negative situations. Let's change these disempowering questions to positive, empowering ones that zoom in and focus on what could be good and right in our lives. The above questions could be changed to as follows:

- Why do I always succeed in the end?
- Why do I lose weight so easily once I put my mind to it?
- Why are opportunities always opening up for me when I least expect them?
- How can I make this situation work for me?
- Why am I lucky enough to have found someone who loves me unconditionally?
- How do I always seem to have everything I need?

Can you "feel" the difference in the second set of questions? Asking yourself more positive questions moves your attention from what you currently lack to what you could have in the future. Changing your mind's focus automatically causes an immediate shift, not only in your being but in your mind and your perspective as well. St. John believes that this practice is the fastest and easiest way to transform your life, and my hat goes off to him for providing us with this very simple yet powerful technique.

An afformation, therefore, is a question that triggers the mind to explore and search out new, creative ways to find solutions to various problems. I highly recommend that you add this method to your reprogramming schedule, asking yourself positive questions regularly throughout the day.

When creating your afformations, use the same tips and guidelines provided for creating your affirmations:

- It should be stated in the present
- It should be stated in the positive
- It should be specific
- It should not be overly specific
- It should not come from a place of desperation or need

Chapter 21

Celebrate Yourself

Remember back to when you were a child, how often you said things like "Look what I did, Mommy," or "Dad, I did this all by myself." When did we learn to stop celebrating ourselves and our accomplishments? As children we could not wait to show off the things we had done, no matter how trivial, and although we should do it for different reasons as adults, that fundamental behavior of celebration and pride should never stop.

Go back and reread part II of this book. Doesn't that give you reason enough to be grateful for and celebrate yourself right there? Look at all your accomplishments, your achievements, things about yourself that, up until now, you have taken for granted. I hope you're beginning to see just how magnificent, resilient, and powerful you really are underneath it all. Look at all the hurdles you have overcome—and now you even have written testament to the fact. Most of the time we are so busy planning the future that we forget to chart and celebrate our progress to date.

Although we should not live in the past, we should never totally forget it. Our past experiences are what has made us who we are today and are the building blocks upon which we will build our tomorrow.

I hope you are feeling as good as I am. You should! It is important to feel successful and accomplished no matter where you are in life. As long as you're breathing you will *always* be a work in progress. That's why success is a journey, not a destination. The more successful you feel right here and now, the more success you stand to receive in the future. Here are six (great) reasons why you should take the time to celebrate yourself on a daily basis:

- Because you actually have many more successes than you do failures in life.
- Because you have learned to give high priority and focus to your shortcomings and mistakes.
- Because most of your achievements go either ignored or unnoticed.
- Because you rarely receive positive feedback for a job well done.
- Because most of the things you do well are so familiar to you that you take them for granted.
- Because celebrating yourself provides a fresh perspective and a shift of emphasis from self-critical thoughts to more positive self-empowering thoughts.

Use a journal every day to record at least three reasons—big or small—why you should celebrate yourself.

It may be for finally cleaning out the spare room, for exercising (extreme) patience with a rude colleague, for filing away the stack of papers that had littered your desk, for finishing the pile of laundry, for calling Aunt Maude, or for taking time out with someone you love. Acknowledging yourself in these situations that would normally be overlooked will help to release negative thought patterns, boost self-confidence, and allow you to feel good about yourself in the now. Keep up this practice, and at the end of each week go back and reread your journal. Celebrate yourself so you can *own* that feel-good, successful vibration in the now!

Note: I suggest you purchase a notebook that is large enough to record both your gratitude and self-celebration entries daily.

Chapter 22

Take Action

So where are we? You've put together a reconditioning program using a special combination of the techniques that have been presented and you are religiously affirming and reprogramming daily in one way or another. "What's next?" you may ask yourself, well…now it's time for action.

In my case, after affirming daily for about a month and asking to be used for service, one night I awoke out of the blue and received the idea for a book called "Mind Right." The title appeared as clear as day, and I immediately jotted it down in my trusty notebook that I keep at my bedside. Right then and there I decided to share everything I had learned over the past few years and was so excited that I couldn't go back to sleep. Inspired? I'd say so!

The idea made perfect sense to me, and it fitted exactly into where I was in life. Having run an inspirational website for the past nine years—during which time I developed an inspirational magazine that later turned into a book entitled *Publish Your First Magazine*—now I could return to my inspirational roots and do exactly what I knew I was born to do. You see, during that period I had toyed with several ideas for my next move: writing a book on business for creative people, developing an app that could help people relate to time differently, creating templates for magazine publishers. Believe me, my friends heard about every one of them as I searched for direction and purpose. But something just *felt* right about creating the book entitled *Mind Right*.

This is an important point for me to emphasize. The idea did not come from a place of fear, lack, anguish, or misery. I had been affirming and meditating daily and as a result was feeling pretty good, and next thing I knew—out of nowhere—my lightning bolt idea arrived.

My point, therefore, is that you should tend to your vibration *first* before taking any type of action. Being at a reasonably high state of vibration will allow ideas and "things" to flow to you more easily—remember what I said about bucking the trend? Never take action from a bad feeling place. Clear up your vibration and patiently wait, because whatever it is will come. But you *must* get out of the way first, as this will definitely *not* be something the ego is responsible for.

If you are reading this now, then you'd better believe that I got out of the way and took action. I immersed myself in various materials, read books, listened to audio, watched DVDs, and absorbed anything I could get my hands on until this book began to take shape. The right resources were always presented to me at exactly the right time. Any questions I had were always answered in one way or another. The whole process actually felt like alchemy!

As for the old adage "follow your heart," it looks like there may be a lot of truth to the saying. In a study published in the *Journal of Alternative and Complementary Medicine* it was found that the heart is much more than the simple pump we think of it as, but is in fact a highly complex system that contains over 40,000 neurons—the same types of cells that make up the majority of the brain—indicating that the heart actually has its own very functional "brain."

Cornell University professor and psychologist Daryl Bem performed a study where subjects were presented with random pictures on a computer. Some were pleasant, picturesque images while others were negative and disturbing. He then used physiological testing equipment to measure the emotional arousal and response time of both the heart and the brain *before* the stimuli were presented. Bem found that, surprisingly enough, the heart responded *before* the image was presented. How could it possibly know what was coming up next when the computer didn't even know? But somehow it was able to intuitively sense an oncoming change, almost as if it could see into the future.

This study indicates that awareness actually begins in the heart and not the (logical) brain as we have previously thought. I hope you can see the magnitude of the implications revealed by this study. The phrase "follow your heart" takes on a whole new meaning once you consider this information.

So be alert to the opportunities that the universe will provide. As you affirm daily, your RAS will seek out and present information relevant to your wants and desires. You'll receive a dominant thought or idea that will eventually nudge you into action. Learn to act on your impulses and intuitions and—most importantly—to trust the guidance that you receive from your heart. These gut-type instincts will *always* guide you to the correct course of action. Before you know it, opportunities will be created and magical synchronistic events will begin to take place that have the power to change your life forever if you allow it.

Once you have that bolt of inspiration, make a bold move right away. Invite the universe to play with you. Let it know you are ready *and* willing. Taking inspired action is the only way you can advance toward the grandest vision that the universe has in store for your life, and believe me, it is bigger than anything you could possibly imagine right here in time.

Thoughts have the ability to bring you your desires, but it is sustained action that will actually allow you to receive them. As soon as you start to take action, you begin to create your future in the now, one step at a time. Be patient and don't try to force the process or hurry it along. Wait until whatever it is feels right. I guarantee you will know—better yet, you will *feel* it!

> **You are only one decision away
> from a totally different life.**
> ~ Author Unknown

Chapter 23

BONUS Chapter: 12 Ways to Stay Motivated on Your Journey

1. Go to <u>www.mindrightbook.com</u> and download your FREE Mind Right Affirmations Quote Book, Mind Right Success Affirmations Screensaver (available in both Mac and PC formats), and Mind Right Success Affirmations CD which provides subliminal affirmations you can groove to. These gifts are from me so enjoy!

2. Hit the Resources section and select the next book you're going to read. It's important that you keep this momentum going, providing you have made it this far.

3. Think of your purpose daily. Keep your purpose alive and at the forefront of your mind. Reflect on your goals daily. Regularly review the new story you have created for yourself by reading over the information gathered in part II. Include a daily practice of observing your vision board for five minutes or more. Really soak in the essence of the images, imagine them to be real and feel the feelings of how it would feel if everything on your board has been accomplished and it represents an accurate depiction of your life right now. Can you *feel* it? Observing your board in this way has the ability to get you amped, as well as increase your energy and general vibe. Plus, you will end up sending very important messages to your subconscious that, as you know, processes in pictures and will most definitely help you on your way to bringing the images to pass.

4. Find other ways to be inspired. Literally become a positive information junkie. Build your arsenal with inspiring books, video, audio programs, music, pictures, affirmations, quotes, sayings, blogs, or websites. You can never have too much positivity in your life! Aim to limit your intake of negative information such as dreary news broadcasts or newspaper stories. Read, watch, or listen to anything that keeps you upbeat and motivated. Make an investment of both time and money in the abundant amount of materials that are available to you. Seek and you will find!

5. Surround yourself with uplifting people. It was Jim Rohn who said, "You are the average of the five people you spend the most time with." This means that what you think and become is largely dependent on those who mostly surround you. Who are your five closest friends and why? It's not good enough to say "I've known her since high school" or "We used to play together as children," not everyone deserves a seat in the front row of your life, some folks need to be waaaaaay in the back somewhere and others not in the theater at all. Life is a theater so choose your audience carefully. Be truthful with yourself, what friends uplift and which ones bring you down? Make a conscious effort to put more time and energy into friends that uplift, and limit interactions with those that don't. It's perfectly fine to love somebody from a distance. Relationships shouldn't be taxing, negative, or leave you feeling down or drained. As much as you are able to, only allow positivity, encouragement, respect, and love into your immediate space. Also, remember that all relationships are a two-way street so be the type of person that you would want to meet or hang out with. You will ultimately attract that which you emanate.

6. Seek support. Very few successful people achieve their goals by themselves. Find individuals who believe in you, can be honest with you, challenge you, provide encouragement, hold you accountable, and who are just genuinely stable and supportive. You're going to need motivating

at times so make sure to keep the numbers of these folks permanently stored in your phone's speed dial list where they can be quickly and easily accessed. Seeking out others with similar aspirations or joining informal support groups can be extremely valuable for staying motivated and keeping you on track. Check out www.meetup.com to find groups who you may share common interests with. And just an FYI…a little trick for when you're feeling less than motivated is to just keep moving until motivation catches up with you. It actually works.

7. Eat and drink to stay healthy. Keep your brain fueled by ensuring the following "brain foods" stay in regular rotation in your diet: salmon, eggs, broccoli, avocado, blueberries, nuts and seeds, dark chocolate, coconut oil, extra virgin olive oil, and green tea. Of course—it almost goes without saying—but stay hydrated. The human brain is comprised of close to 85 percent water and keeping it hydrated will allow you to think faster, increase concentration, balance your mood, boost memory function, and experience greater clarity. Every day aim to drink (about) half a liter of water for every 15kg of your body weight.

8. Exercise. Exercising produces a number of different endorphins which are chemicals that benefit the body by helping to reduce the symptoms of stress, anxiety, and depression; lift moods; boost energy; assist with restful sleep; and enhance the immune system's ability to detect and fend off diseases such as high blood pressure, heart dis-

ease, and diabetes. Physical activity also stimulates brain chemicals that serve to increase brainpower, helping you to think more clearly and be more creative. There's no need for you to become the next Jane Fonda (unless you insist), as experts say that at least 30 minutes of exercise on most days is all you need to stay fit and healthy. You can break the 30 minutes down into shorter sessions of 10 minutes a time, where you aim to exert enough physical activity to increase your heart rate and work up a light sweat. Join a gym, take a brisk walk through your neighborhood, visit the local park, go dancing, walk to work, take the stairs, park on the edge of the mall, or get a Fitbit. Find convenient ways to get your exercise in daily that will make it easier for you to adopt these habits as a permanent way of life.

9. Keep learning. Studies indicate that making a concerted effort to keep learning throughout your lifetime results in higher satisfaction, well-being, and an improved ability to get the most out of life. So keep reading, studying, watching tutorials, researching, or attending classes, conferences, webinars, and seminars. Occasionally switch it up and learn something new about a subject that is outside of your realm or discipline. Whether it's cooking a new dish, picking up a new hobby, or learning a new language, mixing it up allows you to keep it fresh and get the creative juices flowing as you form new neural pathways that serve to awaken different parts of your brain so that you can gain new ideas, associations, insights, and perspectives.

10. Take time out. Taking regular mental breaks is just as important as actually pursuing your goals. Get out in nature, take a nap, meditate, read a book, have fun with family and friends, pet your dog, visit the spa for a massage, or go see a movie. Participate in activities that (temporarily) distract you from your purpose so that you might return refreshed, anew, and raring to go.

11. Keep a journal. Journaling is the simple process of writing down your thoughts and feelings into a trusted notebook, electronic or otherwise. At it's very core, journaling gives permission for you to bare the inner secrets of your soul. It's not only a great tool for personal growth and self-exploration but research has revealed that it's also good for overall stress reduction and emotional healing. Because our minds process about 1000 words per minute, the simple act of writing slows your brain down to 100 words per minute, thereby allowing your thoughts to be recorded on a much deeper and more intimate level. Much like when you hit slow motion while watching a sports clip, events that would normally whiz on by, now have the ability to be viewed with incredible focus, clarity, and detail. It is best advised to write freely, off the cuff. Don't worry about grammar, spelling, sentence structure, or anything else you learned in school. Throw that all out the window! This is your chance to be totally honest and exposed, so free yourself from any type of unnecessary censorship. Upon reflection, you may be surprised by some of your entries. Nothing beats the cognitive benefits

of good old pen and paper but those who prefer digital products should check the DayOne app from www.dayoneapp.com, which is a snazzy personal journal application that can be synced over all of your mobile devices, making it very convenient indeed.

12. Get seven to eight hours in a night. Sleep plays a major role in your mental health. During sleep the neurons in your brain fire nearly as much as while you're awake: consolidating memories, making decisions, clearing out toxins and other wastes, and performing a host of other functions that then allow you to buzz effectively through your day.

When you rewrite the software of your mind,
you change the printout of your life.
~ Elizabeth Powers

Resources

Recommended Reads and Classics

Achor, Shawn.
The Happiness Advantage.
Crown Business, 2010.

Allen, James.
As a Man Thinketh and Other Writings.
Digireads.com, 2005.

Anka, Darryl.
Bashar: Blueprint for Change, A Message from Our Future.
New Solutions Publishing, 1990.

Atkinson, William Walker.
Thought Vibration.
CreateSpace, 2009.

Butler-Bowdon, Tom.
50 Self-Help Classics: 50 Inspirational Books to Transform Your Life.
Nicholas Brealey Publishing, 2003.

Byrne, Rhonda.
The Secret.
Atria Books/Beyond Words, 2007.

Carnegie, Dale.
How to Stop Worrying and Start Living.
Pocket, 2004.

Carpenter, Harry W.
The Genie Within: Your Subconscious Mind-How It Works and How to Use It.
CreateSpace, 2003.

Chopra, Deepak.
The Seven Spiritual Laws of Success.
Amber-Allen Publishing, 2011.

Collier, Robert.
The Secret of the Ages.
Wilder Publications, 2008.

Eker, T. Harv.
Secrets of the Millionaire Mind.
Piatkus Books, 2007.

Ferriss, Timothy.
The 4-Hour Workweek, Expanded and Updated.
Harmony, 2009.

Fried, Jason.
Rework.
Crown Business, 2010,

Gawain, Shakti.
Living in the Light: Follow Your Inner Guidance to Create a New Life and a New World.
World Library Nataraj, 2011.

Goddard, Neville.
Feeling Is the Secret.
Hillary Hawkins Production, 2015.

Grout, Pam.
E-Squared: Nine Do-It-Yourself Energy Experiments That Prove Your Thoughts Create Your Reality.
Hay House Insights, 2013.

Grout, Pam.
E-Cubed: Nine Do-It-Yourself Energy Experiments That Prove Your Thoughts Create Your Reality.
Hay House Insights, 2014.

Haanel, Charles F.
The Master Key System.
Wilder Publications, 2008.

Hawkins, David R.
Power vs. Force.
Hay House, 2013.

Hay, Louis.
You Can Heal Your Life.
Hay House Ltd., 1984.

Hicks, Jerry and Esther.
Ask and It Is Given: Learning to Manifest Your Desires.
Hay House, 2004.

Hicks, Jerry and Esther.
The Amazing Power of Deliberate Intent: Living the Art of Allowing.
Hay House, 2006.

Hicks, Jerry and Esther.
Money and the Law of Attraction: Learning to Attract Wealth, Health, and Happiness.
Hay House, 2008.

Hicks, Jerry and Esther.
The Vortex: Where the Law of Attraction Assembles All Cooperative Relationships.
Hay House, 2009.

Hill, Napoleon.
Think and Grow Rich.
Random House Publishing Group, 1960.

Jeffers, Susan.
Feel the Fear…and Do It Anyway.
Ballantine Books, 2007.

Judkins, Rod
The Art of Creative Thinking: 89 Ways to See Things Differently.
TarcherPerigee, 2016.

Kehoe, John.
Mind Power into the 21st Century.
Zoetic, 2008.

Kleon, Austin.
Steal Like an Artist: 10 Things Nobody Told You About Being Creative.
Adams Media, 2014.

Larson, Christian D.
Your Forces and How to Use Them.
CreateSpace, 2009.

Maltz, Maxwell.
Psycho-Cybernetics.
TarcherPerigee, 2015.

McKenna, Paul.
Change Your Life in Seven Days.
Bantam Press, 2004.

Millman, Dan.
Sacred Journey of the Peaceful Warrior.
HJ Kramer/New World Library, 2004.

Millman, Dan.
Way of the Peaceful Warrior: A Book That Changes Lives.
HJ Kramer, 2006.

Munson, Natasha.
Life Lessons for My Sisters: How to Make Wise Choices and Live a Life You Love!
Hachette Books, 2005.

Murphy, Joseph, Dr.
The Miracle of Mind Dynamics.
Prentice Hall Press, 1972.

Murphy, Joseph, Dr.
The Power of Your Subconscious Mind.
Martino Fine Books, 2009

Nightingale, Earl.
The Strangest Secret.
Laurenzana Press, 2011.

Peale, Norman Vincent, Dr.
The Power of Positive Thinking.
Fireside, 2003.

Rao, Srinivas.
The Art of Being Unmistakable: A Collection of Essays About Making a Dent in the Universe.
CreateSpace Independent Publishing Platform, 2013.

Ravikant, Kamal.
Love Yourself Like Your Life Depends on It.
Love Yourself, 2012.

Redfield, James.
The Celestine Prophecy.
Warner Books, Inc., 1997.

Robbins, Tony.
Unlimited Power, Unleash the Giant Within.
Simon & Schuster, 1991.

Roberts, Jane.
The Nature of Personal Reality: Specific, Practical Techniques for Solving Everyday Problems and Enriching the Life You Know.
Amber-Allen Publishing, 2011.

Ruiz, Don Miguel.
The Voice of Knowledge: A Practical Guide to Inner Peace.
Amber-Allen Publishing, 2004.

Schwartz, David.
The Magic of Thinking Big.
Fireside, 1987.

Smith Orleane, Pia.
Conversations with Laarkmaa: A Pleiadian View of the New Reality.
Balboa Press, 2013.

St. John, Noah.
The Book of Affirmations: Discovering the Missing Piece to Abundant Health, Wealth, Love, and Happiness.
Hay House, Inc., 2014.

Stone, William Clement.
The Success System That Never Fails.
BN Publishing, 2008.

Teodoro, Andrian.
The Power of Positive Energy.
Amazon Digital Services LLC, 2016.

Three Initiates.
The Kybalion: A Study of the Hermetic Philosophy of Ancient Egypt and Greece.
Tarcher, 2008.

Viljoen, Edward.
Bhagavad Gita For Beginners: The Song of God in Simplified Prose.
Amazon Digital Services LLC, 2012.

Voskamp, Ann.
One Thousand Gifts.
Zondervan, 2011.

Walsh, Brian E. PhD.
Unleashing Your Brilliance: Tools & Techniques to Achieve Personal, Professional and Academic Success.
Walsh Seminars, 2005.

Warren, Rick.
The Purpose Driven Life: What on Earth Am I Here For?
Zondervan, 2012.

Wattles, Wallace D.
The Science of Getting Rich.
BN Publishing, 2008.

Williamson, Marianne.
A Course in Weight Loss: 21 Spiritual Lessons for Surrendering Your Weight Forever.
Hay House, 2012.

Williamson, Marianne.
The Law of Divine Compensation: On Work, Money, and Miracles.
HarperCollins Publishers, 2012.

Winfrey, Oprah.
What I Know for Sure.
Flatiron Books, 2014.

Yogananda, Paramhansa.
Autobiography of a Yogi (Reprint of the Philosophical library 1946 First Edition).
Crystal Clarity Publishers, 2003.

Websites for Guided Meditations

AV3X and Digital Meditation
www.av3x.com

Brainsync
www.brainsync.com

Dick Sutphen
www.dicksutphen.com
(I highly recommend the Enhancer and The Zapper.)

Headspace
www.headspace.com

Hayhouse
www.hayhouse.com

Paul McKenna
www.paulmckenna.com

The Unexplainable Store
www.unexplainablestore.com

About the Author

Lorraine Phillips attended Jackson State University where she received an MBA in business administration and a BS in computer science, graduating both programs with honors and distinction. She later went on to earn an AA in graphic design from Bauder College and was elected to *Who's Who Among Students in American Universities & Colleges* for outstanding merit and accomplishments.

Lorraine is a creative information technology professional with over fourteen years' experience in planning, developing, and publishing print, internet, and digital projects. She has been empowering and motivating since the inception of the inspirational website SisterPower.com, which she ran for over ten years before launching *SisterPower* Magazine.

As a dynamic author, speaker, freelancer, and coach, it is her mission to help people achieve their personal and professional dreams. As she puts it in her own words: "It's exactly what I was born to do!"